Gerald Brodribb

Best Wishes

John Langridge

CRICKET AT HASTINGS

THE STORY OF A GROUND

Jim Parks – The Spirit of Festival. Author's Collection

CRICKET AT HASTINGS

The Story of a Ground

by

Gerald Brodribb

SPELLMOUNT LTD.
TUNBRIDGE WELLS, KENT

By the same author:

The English Game, an anthology
All Round the Wicket
Next Man In
The Book of Cricket Verse
Hit for Six
Felix on the Bat
A Yankee Looks at Cricket
The Croucher (Biography of Gilbert Jessop)
Maurice Tate
The Art of Nicholas Felix

In the Spellmount Cricket series:

The Test Match Career of Geoffrey Boycott
by C. D. Clark
The Test Match Career of Sir Jack Hobbs
by Clive Porter
The Test Match Career of Colin Cowdrey
by Derek Barnard
The Test Match Career of Ted Dexter
by Derek Lodge
Cricket Anthology
by Samuel J. Looker

Dedication

*To the memory of the many
great cricketers who have
given such pleasure to the
people of Hastings*

Produced for the Trustees of the
Hastings & St Leonards Central Cricket
& Recreation Ground, Priory Meadow and Hastings Borough Council

First published in the UK in 1989 by
SPELLMOUNT LTD
12 Dene Way, Speldhurst
Tunbridge Wells, Kent TN3 0NX
ISBN 0-946771-93-6
© Trustees Central Cricket and Recreation Ground

British Library Cataloguing in Publication Data
Brodribb, Gerald
    Cricket at Hastings: the story of a ground
    1. England. Cricket grounds
    I. Title
    796.35 '8'06842

ISBN 0-946771-93-6

Text set in 10/12 Times Roman, captions in 8/9 Times Italic
Typeset by Vitaset, Paddock Wood, Kent
Printed in Great Britain by
Staples Printers Rochester Ltd, Kent

Contents

List of Illustrations

Hugh Bartlett, the hero of the 1938 week and captain of Sussex 1947-49. Sussex County Cricket Club

Author's Note

This is the story of how Cricket at Hastings has grown up over the years and found its glory in the Central Ground since its creation in 1864. Apart from its unique position and romantic setting, the ground has the distinction of having enjoyed the appearance of over 625 cricketers who have won Test Match status – 314 winning England caps, and a similar number from overseas.

What countless happy moments this historic ground has provided in the course of some 230 County and Festival matches played here over the last 120 years!

G B

George Cox, who played when aged 54, with 'young' Cox.
Sussex County Cricket Club

Acknowledgements

First, my thanks to all the following great cricketers who have so kindly and readily provided me with their recollections of cricket at Hastings:

L E G Ames
M C Cowdrey
E R Dexter
G H G Doggart

W H V Levett
R G Marlar
A S M Oakman
P W G Parker

Jim Parks
D S Sheppard
D L Underwood

My thanks to Philip Hawkins for detailed comments and valuable advice on the text, to John Manwaring Baines for general help and reading the MS, and also to Tom Land for further reading.

I would like to thank the staff of the Reference Library Hastings, the Curators of the Hastings Museum and Art Gallery, Charles Steggell for the loan of books and information, to the Trustees of the Central Ground (Chairman, Graeme Mounsey) for commissioning me to write the book and for the use of the Library, and in connection with that to Maurice Martin, Vic Pain and Cyril Edwards, also H E H Gabriel.

Thanks and acknowledgements for use of illustrations go to: East Sussex County Library (Hastings Reference Library); Hastings Museum and Art Gallery; Sussex County Cricket Club (Librarian H A Osborne); Barry Funnell; John Hodges; David Padgham; The Trustees of the Central Ground. To the Hastings Council for permission to reproduce the painting of Charles Cundall RA, for use on the jacket. The remainder are from the author's collection.

Special thanks is due to Chris Hawkins for taking many of the photographs.

Although efforts have been made to trace the present copyright holders of photographs, the publishers apologize in advance for any unintentional omission or neglect and will be pleased to insert the appropriate acknowledgement to companies or individuals in any subsequent edition of this book.

Maurice Tate – the perfect action. Author's Collection

1 · Early Cricket at Hastings

The origins of a game can never be traced: it is not until it has reached the stage of being recorded in print that there is any real history. The early random references that turn up are like the tip of an iceberg, and some of these fleeting allusions go back to Elizabethan times.

The first match for which a detailed score has been recorded was one between Kent and An England XI in 1744, and this suggests that the game was now a true public entertainment. The earliest surviving scorecard is that issued by the Sevenoaks Vine Club in 1773, and the publication of Cricket Laws a year later showed that cricket had become a sport with a code that obviously filled the need of its many players.

We know a great deal about the cricketers of Hambledon in the 1770s because they were lucky enough to have a man of letters to write about them, but it did not mean that they were the earliest cricketers; the players of Sevenoaks and of Henfield in West Sussex are among those who date back to even earlier times. There is abundant proof that by the mid-eighteenth century cricket was established in the south of England almost on a county basis, though the claims of a team to represent the county were somewhat extravagant. The grandiose titles were largely an advertising ploy to attract the crowds, and the crowds certainly came to watch.

It is probable that cricket was first played at Hastings as a result of the enthusiasm of James, the son of the distinguished John Collier, who was the town's most eminent citizen until his death in 1760. James wrote to his father in July 1745 about a great game of cricket he had just seen between Kent and All England on Bromley Common; he said he hoped soon to tell those at Hastings all about it. It cannot be by chance that a map of the Collier estates dated 1749-50 shows a plot of 7 acres marked as 'The Cricket Field'; this is now covered by the present Priory Road. It is reasonable to believe that this cricket field was established as a result of James Collier's enthusiasm for the game.

The next reference to Hastings cricket comes in a lease dated 1785 when 'the cricketing field' is mentioned as part of the America Ground which then covered what is now Carlisle Parade and Robertson Street. In the days before the great sea-wall was begun in 1930, the foreshore ran almost up to the line of the houses. There was no real ownership, and this swampy area was occupied by squatters. It was not until 1850 that there was any attempt to develop it. Lord Carlisle, the chief commissioner of Woods and Forests, now appropriated the land; hence the name 'Carlisle Parade'. The America Ground cannot have provided much of a cricket field, and was more generally connected with smuggling.

The earliest date of a game in which Hastings cricketers are involved is 23 September 1790 when on Westfield Down a team called Hastings and Guestling (with 5 from Tenterden) played a mixed team from Bexhill, Battle, Sedlescombe and Northiam (with 5 from Rolvenden). No result is known of this odd match, but the fact that it is reported suggests that there could have been many other unrecorded games at that time. The mere selection of these hybrid teams implies some powers of organisation.

After a long gap of silence the first recorded game played at Hastings was on 24 July 1815. To quote a report: 'On Monday a match of cricket was played on the field next the Garrison at Hastings between eleven scientific players of Breed, and eleven of the same description, residents of Hastings, which terminated greatly in favour of the former: thus it appears, every cock has not at all times the good fortune to crow upon his own territories.' The Garrison was the barracks at Halton near the Church, and the field was probably that marked on the 1749-50 map of the Collier estates. In the following year there was a game on Bulverhythe Salts between the Gentlemen of Hastings and the Webster Battle Club which produced scores of: Hastings 67 & 47, Battle 40 & 35.

Cricket on the East Hill 1825. E. Sussex County Library (Hastings Reference Library)

The next two decades produced reports of about 30 cricket matches, many of them played on the East Hill, near Rocklands. There is a woodcut showing play there dated 1825. In 1822 four Gentlemen of Hastings contested four Gentlemen of Bexhill in home and away games, and other names of opponents found are Ninfield, Sedlescombe, Battle, Beckley, Hailsham, Wartling, Appledore, Rye and Fairlight. It seems strange that *The Brighton Herald* should bother to report a game at

16

The great Victor Trumper relaxes in a goat-cart trip along the sands at Hastings in 1905.
David Frith

Hastings in 1825 between 'a Grocer and Four friends', or one in 1827 between 'Old and Young Tradespeople'. To us today the scores seem very low, for example, in 1824: Battle 27 & 109 v Hastings 44 & 46, and in the return game a week later: Hastings with 25 & 47 lost to Battle 27 & 47-5. The reason for such low scoring was the very rough unprepared pitches and the need for all hits to be run out with virtually no boundaries. The frequent reports of such games suggest not only an increasing number of cricketers, but also of those interested enough to want to read about the games in the papers. Most of the reports appear very soon after the match, often next day.

By the mid-1830s there is evidence of challenge matches: in 1837 we hear of a single-wicket three-a-side match for 'a good supper and one dozen of wine' at Priory Brooks Ground, a ground seldom mentioned but probably near the area of the present Central Ground. A certain Mr Clements was top scorer with innings of 2 & 7 and his bowling was 'superior' because he took all six wickets. One of the opposition, W Yates, 'did beyond what was expected of him' by taking 5 wickets. In the same year the Hastings Wellington Club challenged the Old Battle Club at Priory Brooks for 22 sovereigns a side. The money motive was beginning to appear, and we see it again two years later when the St Leonards Club challenged that of Hastings for 11 sovereigns, adding: 'If

17

this should not suit the wishes of the Hastings Gents, 7 of the St Leonards will play 7 of the Hastings. All hits. A sovereign a man.'

In June 1839 a match took place at Hastings between Hastings Old Club and the village of Chalvington (a few miles from Polegate), and its importance is that it was reported in the *Sussex Weekly Advertiser*, *The Brighton Herald*, the *Brighton Gazette*, and later in *MCC Scores and Biographies*. Why? It seems to be the first local match of which was given a full account of play as well as the scores. The two clubs were 'testing their powers of mastery in the Noble game of cricket'. Fierce criticism was directed at one of the Chalvington bowlers who seemed to be (illegally) raising his hand above the level of the shoulder: 'This overhand bowling, otherwise throwing, has destroyed those beautiful hits which in days of yore elicited the admiration of spectators.' The writer goes on to say with some degree of prophecy of present times: 'Now, a man is scarcely safe even when he is enveloped in wadding, which a gunshot would not penetrate!'

It is difficult to realise today the controversy which lasted from 1835, when a man was permitted to raise his arm to waist level, to 1864, when he could at last legally deliver the ball as now, at overarm level. It took some 30 years for this fundamental change in law, and all the time lively argument prevailed. Will it take another 30 years before today's teams, packed with would-be fast bowlers, are persuaded to speed up their over-rate and get on with the game 'as in days of yore'?

The match against Chalvington was a close win for Hastings, who made 110 and 63 (including in all 13 wides and 50 byes) against their opponents' totals of 78 and 105, including 9 wides and 27 byes. Thus, nearly 30% of the runs came from wides and byes. The new style of so-called 'throwing' bowling gave away many runs, since it is not easy to bowl fast round-arm and keep on target.

Yet another form of challenge in 1838 was the playing for 'a grand silver cup valued at 25 guineas' between an XI from the parishes of All Saints and St Clements against those from the Castle and St Leonards. The first innings ended in a tie at 55 runs each, but St Leonards won in the end by 4 wickets. In the usual instant return match a week later St Clements got their revenge.

Next year in a match between two veteran local teams called The Corinthians and The Masticators, heavy rain held up play in the afternoon which disappointed 'hundreds of the admirers of the noble game', but there was time later for the Masticators to score 60 and 26, and the Corinthians, having scored 70, needed only 17 runs to win. To quote the report: 'It was now dark, but nothing daunted, they again took bat in hand.' Wickets fell rapidly, but with the Corinthians needing 2 runs to win with one wicket in hand, the game had to come to an end. The players were totally unable to see each other. No light meters needed here.

18

I have recorded this wide range of games to show how cricket was developing in the area, but there was no representative town cricket club, many of the teams already mentioned belonging to local societies who raised a side for some special challenge. However, in 1840 the first Hastings cricket club was formed, and it played on what was known as Thwaites' field, later known as Breed's Field, on the West Hill, not far from the cricket field noted on the Collier map of 1749-50. The field was named after Edward Thwaites (b 1801) who had been a member of the celebrated Hawkhurst Club, and later came to Hastings where he was in business as a tallow chandler. He had played once for England against 'The Bs' in a match at Lords in 1825. In the following year he appeared in a match for Hastings (assisted by Fielder and Sawyer) against a local three-some at Benenden for a stake of £40 – a fair sum of money. One of the Benenden three, J G Wenman, was a cousin of the famous E G Wenman, the Kent player. He stayed at the wicket for nearly two days, and almost reached a century – a very rare feat.

On 9 July 1840 the new Hastings Club, assisted by James Lillywhite, played Tunbridge Wells (assisted by Alfred Mynn and Box) at the Thwaites' Ground on West Hill, and Hastings won by 15 runs. The return match at Tunbridge Wells also provided a victory. The importance of these two fixtures is that many of the top players of the day, Fuller Pilch, Mynn, Lillywhite, Box, E G Wenman and W Martingell took part. Seldom has such a galaxy of the great been connected with local cricket.

Part of poster of cricket on the East Hill 1842. Sussex County Cricket Club (Librarian H A Osborne)

The new club began to play further afield, and we read of games against Brighton on the West Hill in 1843. One of the opposing team was a certain C H Gausden, who played 7 games professionally for Sussex after his debut in 1847. He was responsible for the opening of the Brunswick Ground in 1848. He later moved to St Leonards, became part of the estate agent firm of Gausden and Dawson, and eventually became Mayor of Hastings in 1873, 1876 and 1878. His interest in cricket was very helpful.

Cricket was increasingly popular in the 1840s, and the time was ripe for the creation of Clarke's ALL ENGLAND XI which for many years toured the country playing mostly teams of local XXIIs. This team did much to promote a far wider interest in cricket and people flocked to the matches. Later there were other rival touring teams which helped to establish cricket as a major pastime and spectacle. 'The English Game' had arrived.

In Hastings in May 1856 a new club, the Priory Club, was formed and it was agreed that because of the difficulty of getting time off from work, players should practice on the West Hill every Monday, Wednesday and Friday at 5.30 am. Before long a rival team called East End Amateurs challenged the Priory Club, the match being played from 5.30 until the call of the day's work. This devotion to the game and sense of duty so much aroused the admiration of the employers that they arranged for a return match on a Tuesday afternoon in work time – a great concession. Henry Phillips, a local hero of whom more later, tells how young players would arrange to be called for this early practice by having a string tied to their toes left hanging out of the window to be pulled by the one chosen to wake them. One early call once went wrong: 'On one occasion this led to a very early practice indeed, for the boy who pulled the cord woke up by moonlight and thought it was the right time to rise, so he dressed, went out, and pulled the strings. The result was that about half a dozen boys went up to practise and before long were left in the dark, because the moon began to go down. They had got up just after midnight!'

We have read how others, including the great Australians, Trumper, Macartney and Bardsley, would get up early and practise before breakfast. I wonder how many ambitious young cricketers of today would do likewise.

In 1857 the Sussex County Cricket Club was reformed and on 10 and 11 September a Sussex team played the MCC on the old racecourse ground at Bulverhythe (at the bottom of Filsham Road) – the first time a county team had appeared in the district. John Lillywhite and George Hooker bowled unchanged for Sussex in both MCC innings, and helped the county to a 70 run win, the scores being Sussex 91 and 106, MCC 58 and 69. Hooker was at that time engaged by the newly formed East Sussex Club, and in the following year when playing for the Gentlemen of Sussex XXII against the great United England XI on the racecourse ground, he

20

GRAND MATCH OF CRICKET

20 GENTLEMEN OF

SUSSEX,

AND TWO BOWLERS,

UNITED ELEVEN OF

ALL

ENGLAND

18th, 19th, and 20th August, 1859,

On the East Sussex Cricket Ground, St. Leonards

SUSSEX — First innings		Second Innings	
J. H. Hale, esq. run out	4	run out	15
G. King, Esq. b by Caffyn	2	b Caffyn	11
W. Napper, Esq. c and b by Grundy	0	c Carpenter b Wisden	0
E. B. Fawcett Esq. c Hearne, b Caffyn	2	b Lockyer	8
F. Thomas, Esq. c Wisden, b Caffyn	4	b Griffith	4
H. Stent, Esq., c Carpenter, b Grundy	0	c Carpenter b Griffith	6
W. P. Beecham, Esq., c Caffyn, b Wisden	6	b Griffith	4
Mr. Stubberfield, b Caffyn	28	c Hearne b Griffith	26
H. M. Curteis, Esq. c Hearne, b by Caffyn	5	run out	2
Mr. Hoad, b by Carpenter	0	b Griffith	3
Mr. Hooker c Wells b Caffyn	3	b Griffith	4
E. Hume, Esq., run out	3	c Wells b Wisden	3
J. Beasley, Esq. c and b Caffyn	0	b Griffith	0
Captain Parish R. N. b by Carpenter	3	run out	0
E. Follett, Esq., b by Wisden	0	run out	0
V. B. Crake, Esq., b Wisden	0		
W. Watts, Esq. l b w, b by Carpenter	12	run out	10
A. R. W. Day, Esq. c Carpenter, b wisden	7		
A. Knox, Esq. b Carpenter	0	b Griffith	4
H. Wilson, Esq, c Wells, b wisden	1		
G. T. Lawrence, Esq., not out	0	c Griffith b Grundy	5
H. Bethune, Esq. b Carpenter	1		
No balls, Wides, Byes, 3	3	No balls, Wides, Byes, 6	
Total	92	Total	

UNITED ELEVEN. First Innings		Second Innings.	
John Lillywhite c Napper, b Hooker	5		
Mortlock, b Stubberfield	3		
Hearne, c and b Stubberfield	2		
Wells, b Hooker	10		
A. Infelix, Esq. c and b Stubberfield	1		
Carpenter, c and b Hooker	1		
Lockyer c Fawcett b Hooker	18		
Caffyn, not out	35		
Wisden, st Hoad b Stubberfield	6		
Grundy, run out	11		
Griffith, c Day b Hooker	0		
No balls, Wides, 1 Byes, 4	5	No balls Wides Byes	
Total	97	Total	

Printed on the ground at the fall of every wicket, by F. Thomson.

Sussex v All England at Bulverhythe, St Leonards 1859. Sussex County Cricket Club

took 16 of the 20 United wickets that fell – a remarkable feat. Lord Sheffield of Sheffield Park and originator of the Sheffield Shield in Australia, played in that match. The United England XI match became a regular fixture.

In 1861, after the East Sussex Club was dissolved, the Hastings and St Leonards United Club was formed and attracted huge crowds to its ground on the East Hill near Rocklands; but the site was becoming dangerous. To quote a report: 'The balls flying about in all directions, and actually striking some of the visitors.'

In 1862 yet another itinerant touring team had been started, Julius Caesar's NEW ALL ENGLAND XI, and it met the Hastings United XXII and lost by 3 runs amid great excitement among the many raucous partisans. It was clear that although the East Hill ground was inconveniently situated and some way from the centre, cricket was now a great attraction to the public, who at that time had few other diversions. There was need for a new ground in the town, easier to reach and offering better control of the game. It was soon to be found, and this opened up a new chapter in the history of cricket at Hastings.

One of the painted glass windows in old Pavilion of 1884.
Author's Collection

2 · The History of the Central Ground

The Central Ground covers what was once a natural harbour, and in an early map of 1746 the area is marked as 'the Haven'. Though the harbour silted up, a wide stream continued to run across the area and flowed under a wooden bridge in the town centre until in 1839 the stream was enclosed in an underground culvert. The ground lies at sea level and from time to time has been subject to severe flooding: in the spring of 1913 water covered the ground to a depth of 2 feet – enough for boats – and at one later flood H Gabriel recalls how Sir Charles Kirkpatrick, a keen supporter, once dived off the railings in front of the pavilion and swam about there. Before the great sea-wall was built in the late 1920s the

22

Cricket near Gensing Manor, St Leonards c1860, London Road in the background.
John Hodges

distance between the cricket square and the foreshore was less than 200 yards. There cannot be a first-class ground in any town, anywhere else, that is more centrally situated.

The Priory Meadow was connected with the Priory Farm near the site of the former Augustinian Priory, and was part of extensive lands belonging to the Cornwallis estate. The Hon Stanley Cornwallis (later Lord Cornwallis) captained Kent in the 1920s and played at Hastings in county matches.

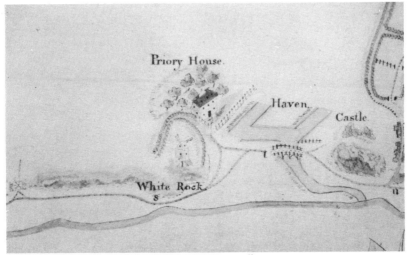

Extract from Samuel Kant's map of 1746. Barry Funnell

In the early 1860s the Hastings United Club, now consisting of some 50 members, decided that the East Hill ground was no longer adequate; they looked round for somewhere more accessible, and considered the Priory Meadow as a possible site for a new ground. At the same time there was a rumour that the area might be sold for building. A public meeting was held and a committee formed that worked so quickly that within a fortnight they had reported back that the meadow would be available at a rent of £25 per annum, but that it would cost £300 to level, drain and returf the two acres in the middle. In a few months a total of £610 had been raised, and work on the ground was started immediately. It was ready for play by the end of the summer of 1864.

The new ground was such a success that five years later at the annual meeting of members and subscribers it was resolved that the committee should approach the representatives of the Cornwallis estate to see if they might be willing to sell the ground to the club. There was some delay in reply because the owners were still uncertain about the use of that area for building, but the committee finally persuaded them to retain it, since a cricket and recreation ground would be beneficial to all parties and a great asset to the town. An offer was made and a scheme for management was included in a Bill which had to be placed before parliament as part of the Cornwallis Estates Act of 1870.

The accepted price was £5,000 and as a result of a public meeting on 5 February 1872 the subscription list reached £3,180. The Cornwallis estate accepted a down payment of £3,000, the balance of £2,000 to be left on mortgage at an interest rate of 4%. This mortgage remained outstanding until it was finally paid off in the 1950s with money resulting from the new Queen's Road Development.

Severe flooding in March 1913. E. Sussex County Library (Hastings Reference Library)

BOROUGH OF HASTINGS.

ROSS, MAYOR.

Notice is Hereby Given,
That in pursuance of a Requisition
for the purpose, a Public Meeting
of the Inhabitants of the Borough
of Hastings, will be held at the
Assembly Room at the Castle Hotel,
in the said Borough, on Monday,
the 8th day of January inst., at half-
past Seven o'clock in the evening
precisely, "To take into consideration
"the best means of raising the money
"required to purchase the Central
"Cricket and Recreation Ground."

By the Mayor,

MEADOWS,

Town Clerk.

Hastings, 1st January, 1872.

PARSONS & COUSINS, STEAM PRINTERS, HASTINGS AND RYE.

Notice calling for meeting about the Trust 1872. Trustees of the Central Ground

On 7 August 1872 the Trust Deed came into being and its conditions
required the trustees of the ground to hand over some strips of land to
form highways which became part of South Terrace and Queen's Road,
then known as Meadow Road. A strip on the south-west side was handed
over to form Station Road, and there was an obligation to enclose the

25

Sir Thomas Brassey celebrates his election as MP 1869. E. Sussex County Library
(Hastings Reference Library)

ground with a wall. It was also laid down that the trustees 'shall allow the ground to be used by the inhabitants and visitors of the Borough of Hastings and neighbourhood as a pleasure ground and a place of recreation.' The ground, but not the buildings on it, was to be open to the public one day in every week (not Sunday) and it could be requisitioned by the Mayor of Hastings to be used 'as a place of public meeting for any lawful purpose for two days, and two days only, in the course of any six consecutive months.' It is said that the last time this ground was requisitioned was in 1951 when the Queen (then Princess Elizabeth) came to Hastings to receive the Deeds of the Castle and Glens and to hand them over to the Corporation of Hastings. So the Trust was formed and the trustees were now faced with the problem of managing the ground and raising the money for its upkeep. The Trust is a private concern and the Town Council has never contributed to it except for the loan of deck chairs and a small grant to cover extra labour costs when a first-class match was on. The Trust had great responsibility for administration as there was always a lack of ready income, partly owing to a shortage of ground subscribers; even in better years the takings seldom exceeded £250, so other means of raising money had to be considered. In the early

26

days we hear of Evening Fêtes, a Health Exhibition in 1889, an Archery Club, circuses, athletic meetings on Bank Holidays, including a race by errand boys riding their delivery bicycles; these sports meetings were enhanced by a massive organ (though this brought complaints); once there was a suggestion to use the new wall on the Queen's Road side as a mounting for advertisement boards, but this was regarded as 'distasteful'.

In the early 1890s great argument arose about letting part of the ground for football which 'seemed now to be displacing cricket as a popular pursuit'. Some were in favour of football and pointed out that it was a recreation as well as a cricket ground; others thought it would be too damaging to the turf. A compromise was to make the footballers stop play by the end of February, to which they objected. A certain amount of football was however played, there are some photographs of it, and my father told me he used to play there. Another suggestion for use was the creation of lawn tennis courts, but it was decided to wait and see how this new game developed.

On other occasions the ground was officially called into use for hustings during elections; it was hired as a drilling ground for the Cinque Port Volunteers – the Countess Waldegrave kindly paying the fee; it was the scene of drumhead services and of the recruiting campaigns for the Boer War and the First World War.

In much later years lawn tennis courts were laid out for the public with a huge tournament in the late summer, there were push ball contests, youth rallies were held and a bowling green was created in the south-west corner, which for a time became the headquarters of the Hastings Bowls Club. Another small source of income was the letting of the space next to the Town Hall (where the Maidstone buses once used to operate) to the Wallis Arthur Concert Party, who put up a large tent for their entertainment.

Election Hustings: Nomination Day 1865. Hastings Museum & Art Gallery

HASTINGS AND ST. LEONARDS

Cricket and Recreation Ground.

➤✳ 1892 ✳◄

LIST OF CRICKET MATCHES & FÊTES

DATE	MATCH			TIME
Wednesday, May 18th	Alexandra	v.	South Saxons	1.30
Tuesday, May 24th	Alexandra 2nd 11	v.	University School	2
Wednesday, May 25th	Alexandra	v.	Silverhill	1.30
*Monday, June 6th	**BANK HOLIDAY FÊTE**			2
Wednesday, June 8th	Hastings Club	v.	Eastbourne	11
Wednesday, June 15th	Alexandra	v.	Willingdon	11
Wednesday, June 15th	Athletic Club Evening		Meeting	6
Friday, June 17th	Alexandra 2nd 11	v.	Highbury House	2
Monday, July 4th	Hastings Police	v.	East Sussex Police	11
Tuesday, July 5th	Alexandra 2nd 11	v.	University School	2
Wednesday, July 6th	Rovers	v.	Bexhill	11
Wednesday, July 6th	St. Leonards Cycling		Club Evening Fête	6
Friday, July 8th	Hastings Club	v.	Willesden Park	11
Monday, July 11th	Stewart's Old Boys' Match			11
Tuesday, July 12th	**ALEXANDRA**	**v.**	**RICHMOND TOWN,** (BENEFIT MATCH)	11
Wednesday, July 13th	Rovers	v.	Rye	11
Friday, July 15th	Hastings Club	v.	Cinque Ports Wanderers (LONDON)	11
Wednesday, July 20th	Hastings Club	v.	Brighton Brunswick	11
Wednesday, July 20th	Athletic Club Evening		Meeting	6
*Monday, July 25th	**ALLIANCE ATHLETIC CLUB FÊTE**			2
Wednesday & Thursday, July 27 & 28	Hastings Club	v.	Hornsey	11
*Monday, August 1st	**BANK HOLIDAY FÊTE**			2
Wednesday, August 3rd	Rovers	v.	Silverhill	11
*Wednesday, August 10th	**ATHLETIC CLUB ANNUAL FÊTE**			2
Thursday & Friday, Aug. 11 & 12	Hastings Club	v.	County Club and Ground	11
Tuesday, August 16th	Alexandra	v.	Charlton Park	11
Wednesday, August 17th	Alexandra 2nd 11	v.	East End	2
Thursday & Friday, August 18 & 19	Hastings Club	v.	Chiswick Park	11
Tuesday, August 23rd	Alexandra	v.	Battle	11
Wednesday & Thursday, Aug. 24 & 25	**HASTINGS CLUB**	**v.**	**M.C.C. & GROUND** (BENEFIT MATCH)	11
Friday, August 26th	Alexandra 2nd 11	v.	Bexhill	2
Wednesday, August 31st	Hastings Club	v.	Folkestone Town	11
Wednesday, August 31st	Athletic Club Evening		Meeting	6
Monday, September 5th	Police	v.	Coastguards	11

CRICKET WEEK

*September 8th, 9th, & 10th	**NORTH**	v.	**SOUTH**	12
*September 12th, 13th, & 14th	**GENTLEMEN**	v.	**PLAYERS**	12
Thursday, September 15th	Ground Superintendent's (*Manwaring*) Benefit Match			11
Wednesday, September 21st	Alexandra 2nd 11	v.	East End Club	2

*5/- TICKETS WILL NOT ADMIT TO THESE MATCHES.

Programme of Diverse Events 1892. Sussex County Cricket Club

28

A Push-Ball Tournament in 1907. John Hodges

By the late 1930s the Trust became more comfortable financially with increased subscribers, and there was the constant use of pitches and nets for clubs, schools and others. In 1949 it was claimed by the Trust that this was the most heavily used first-class cricket ground in Great Britain. All this activity was necessary to cover the costs to keep the ground going.

To return to the story of the creation of the ground. By the summer of 1864 the ground was ready enough to welcome the United All England XI in a match against the Hastings United XXII when they came to Hastings on 29, 30, 31 August. This inaugural match was recorded in MCC *Scores and Biographies*, and was memorable for the great hitting of Ben Griffiths which is described later in the section on Big Hits. Here is a report of this historic match:

'The first "grand Match" on the new ground in the Priory Meadow opened under very favourable auspices . . . The All England Eleven expressed approval of the new ground, which it is thought will be in first-rate order next season. Considerable pains had been taken under Mr Barham's directions to get a good spot for the wickets and a very fair piece of turf was obtained for the play. Joint arrangements of the Hastings United Club and the Recreation Ground Committee are very suitable for the occasion.

'Numerous tents were provided – one specially for ladies – beside a wooden structure, and a large number of stools added to the comfort of visitors. The advantage of the Central Ground in point of convenience was shown in the presence of a large number of fashionable equipages and equestrians.'

There is also a report of another match on the new ground played on 3 October 1864 between Eleven Visitors of Hastings and St Leonards and the Hastings Club. The Visitors made 75 and 50 and Hastings 84.

Lawn Tennis Tournament c1910. David Padgham

The official opening of the ground was not until 18-19 April 1865 in a match between Eleven of Hastings and Eleven of St Leonards. Among the players were Thomas Parkin, the Hastings cricket historian, the brothers Albert and Henry Phillips and R A H Mitchell, an outstanding batsman, whose first-class appearances were limited by his being a master at Eton College. It was a big day for Hastings when at the end of the season of 1865 a three-day match was played on 4, 5, 6 September, between the counties of Sussex and Kent – the first county match to be played at Hastings. This game was not sponsored by the County Committees, but was a special fixture arranged as a way of advertising the new ground, and giving the locals a chance of seeing county cricketers in action. Though James Lillywhite clean bowled the first two Kent batsmen

Southern Counties Archery Meeting 1933. Hastings Museum & Art Gallery

30

with the first two balls of the game, the scores were Kent 128 and 179 and Sussex 142 and 112-6, and the match was drawn. A report states: 'This was another great game drawn owing to the system of delay now generally adopted: the play altogether in the 3 days did not occupy 14 hours.' In other words, the late starts and prolonged intervals seriously cut down playing time, but the match proved that Hastings could now provide a ground fit for three-day matches.

Many people had worked very hard to bring the new ground into shape, but it was still rather bleak and in October 1866 the *Observer* included this appeal from the well-known school master and the Hon Sec of the ground, John Banks, asking for help over planting trees round the ground. Here is a quotation from his appeal poem called '*Trees, Trees, Trees*':

> If you have any trees to spare, why, we can plant them round
> About the Hastings Central Cricket and Recreation Ground.
> We've levelled, drained and fenced it too, and
>   Spent a lot of money,
> In making what was once a swamp
>   A field both green and sunny.

A hundred years later, Len Creese, the famous Hastings groundsman, beautified the Central Ground by introducing many new trees, a benefaction he later repeated at Hove.

In 1868 the Australian Aboriginal team – the first overseas team ever to tour England – played a three-day match against a Hastings XI. It remained unfinished partly because play ended early on the third day to allow time for the Aborigines to exhibit their skills in catching, whip cracking, dodging cricket balls and boomerang throwing. They also took part in the athletics, and more than 3,000 people turned up to see them on this last day. It was not until 1988 that an Aboriginal team again toured England.

Soon after the setting up of the Trust in 1872 the Hastings United Club now became the Hastings and St Leonards Cricket Club. The next year the Hastings cricketers played the MCC at Lords, but with scores of 85 and 125 lost by an innings to the MCC total of 344. A return match was played on 28-29 August on the Central Ground. On the Friday 'owing to the terrible rain that fell during the morning, fresh wickets were cut.' During the innings of Mr Alberga (MCC) his handkerchief blew from his belt, and twined round the wicket, but did not remove the bails. This fixture with the MCC was a feather in the cap of the Hastings Club, because MCC did not at that time play many provincial matches. The reputation of Hastings cricket was spreading. It is interesting to see what

CRICKET!

A MATCH WILL BE PLAYED ON THE

Central Ground,

HASTINGS, ON

WEDNESDAY & THURSDAY,

AUGUST 18th and 19th, 1886,

Between TWELVE of the

M.C.C. & GROUND

And TWELVE of the

Hastings & St. Leonards C.C.

M. C. C. and Ground.	Hastings & St. Leonards C.C
G. H. WOOD	H. PIGG
C. W. FOLEY	J. PHILLIPS
L. G. ARBUTHNOT	W. J. RANSOM
E. A. PARKE	P. H. MARTINEAU
H. K. AVORY	A. PHILLIPS
J. H. FARMER	T. PARKIN
P. COLES	G. H. ELVIDGE
P. R. PAPILLON	C. LAVENDER
H. FREEMAN	A. CLARK
T. MOORE	C. H. YOUNG
RYLOTT	R. STANDEN
PICKETT	KIDMAN

Wickets pitched at 11.30 o'clock each day.

A Luncheon will be provided on the Ground at 2 o'clock by Mr. T. Turner, of the Globe Hotel, Tickets 2/6.

ADMISSION, 6d.   CARRIAGES, 2s. 6d.   BATH CHAIRS, 1s,

Subscribers' Tickets not available for this Match.

RANDLE, Queen's Printing Works, Hastings.

Poster of MCC v Hastings and St Leonards 1886.
Sussex County Cricket Club

sort of entrance charges were made at that time. A notice of 1874 says: 'Admission, each day, 6d. Carriages, 2s 6d. Equestrians, 1s. Refreshments were available: 'A COLD COLLATION will be provided on the Ground at Two o'clock, and refreshments supplied by Mr T Turner, of the Globe Hotel, Hastings.'

Quaint matches were still an attraction and in 1874 a two-day match between One Arm and One Leg took place at 'Recreation Meadow, Meadow Road' an odd term for the ground. One Arm, by scoring 150 and 146 against One Leg 117 and 175, won a very close match by 4 runs. Other unusual games included a Clown's match on 1875, an Electric Light match in 1883 and a Ladies match in 1891. At about that time a ladies club called the Crows operated at Crowhurst Park, the home of the Papillons.

In 1875, in one of several appearances, the United South XI came to face an XVIII of Hastings and District. The game was dominated by an innings by W G Grace, who scored 210 out of his side's total of 359. Hastings scored 126 and 102-12. During his innings WG made an out of the ground hit which was measured at 118 yards hit to pitch. Perhaps this went in the direction of the new Town Hall, which was being built in the south corner of the ground. We tend to forget the problems of making big scores when opposed by so many fielders.

By this time the itinerant teams started by Clarke in 1846 were beginning to dissolve, partly through the rise of county-based cricket, but they had all done a very good job in spreading the game.

In 1878 came a touring team of another kind, the first visit of the Australians to England. Hastings was lucky enough to get on the list of

The first Australian touring team of 1878
(standing) C Bannerman, H F Boyle, J Mc C Blackman, F R Spofforth,
? W Midwinter, G H Bailey, F E Allan, ? Umpire
(sitting) Gibbs (Asst Sec), W L Murdoch, D W Gregory (capt), T Horan, J Conway (Sec)
(on ground) A C Bannerman, T W Garrett

The first Australian team of 1878. Trustees of the Central Ground.

33

fixtures, when on 26, 27, 28 August the visitors, with a score of 260, easily defeated the Hastings total of 131 and 82. In the Hastings second innings the Demon Bowler, Spofforth, was quite unplayable. 'With the pitch suiting him to a nicety', he produced an analysis of 33-12-39-12; in the course of 5 overs (4 balls each), he took 9 wickets for 5 runs, including a feat which 'entitled him to a New Hat at the expense of the Club' when he

ANALYSIS OF THE BOWLING OF THE FIRST INNINGS.

BOWLER.	RUNS FROM EACH OVER.	WIDE BALLS.	NO BALLS.	RUNS.	WICKETS	OVERS.
1 2 F. R. Spofforth	M w . / ' / ' MM , M ' w w MM . M '	0	1	39	12	33
3 4 F. E. Allan	M . 2 M . w M / 14 . / M . 2 MMMMM M# MM 2	0	0	25	4	22
5						
6 J. R. Garratt	MMMMM	0	0	0	0	5
7 H. F. Boyle	/ MM . w	0	0	4	1	5-2
8						

Detail of Spofforth's analysis of 12-33 v Hastings 1878. Trustees of the Central Ground

clean bowled 3 batsmen with consecutive balls. This is one of the earliest references to a 'Hat Trick'. Among the Hastings team were such players as Lord Harris, Mr F Penn, the Hon Ivo Bligh, Mr C A Absolom, Mr W Carless (founder of the Hastings Festival) and E J McCormick (then aged only 15). There were huge crowds and a profit was made of £70. Two years later the Australians came again and Hastings did better with scores of 245 and 176 against the Australians' scores of 186 and 60-3. James Phillips scored 29 and 26: we shall hear more of him later.

1880 also saw a new fixture, the first county match arranged under county auspices, but Leicester, the opponents, were not yet of first-class status, and Sussex won easily, thanks partly to a fine score of 68 by the local youngster, McCormick. The authorities now realised the potential of county cricket at Hastings, but it was not until 1895 – fifteen years later – that annual county matches were played. In the meantime the festival had done much to raise the general standard of cricket in the district. The Club had three professionals, and ran two, and sometimes three, sides every Wednesday, the town's half-day. Sometimes, four teams could appear on the ground on the same day and in the long evenings some games would start at 6.30 and go on till dark. There were many attractive club games and fine cricket, but none more exciting than an innings played by W J Ford for MCC v the South Saxons at the Central Ground in 1883. Going in first, he was fourth out at 147 for a score of 113 made in 80 minutes. The side owed him much and was all out for 163. Ford, one of the biggest hitters ever known, hit one six into the third storey of a house, and he also hit 19 fours, many of which were probably over the ropes and would have counted six nowadays.

(2d.) **AUTHORISED CRICKET CARD.** (2d.)

Australians v. Hastings and District.

Monday, Tuesday, & Wednesday, Aug. 30th, 31st, & Sept. 1st.

Eighteen of Hastings and District.

J. Phillips (Captain) c Bonnor, b Palmer	29	run out	26
E. J. McCormick .. b Palmer	2	run out	35
W. W. Reeve c Bonnor, b Alexander	61	b Palmer	3
W. Langley c Palmer, b Boyle	0	st Jarvis, b Boyle	7
L. Howell b M'Donnell	10	c Moule, b Palmer	6
A. H. Stratford c Groube, b M'Donnell	15	b Alexander	8
A. Phillips c Moule, b Palmer	17	c Moule, b Alexander	10
W. Draper run out	17	b Palmer	0
G. Spillman c Alexander, b Boyle	23	c Jarvis, b Alexander	25
T. J. Green b M'Donnell	2	c Slight, b Alexander	0
A. W. Soames c Bonnor, b Palmer	7	b Palmer	3
G. A. Von Reischach c Murdoch, b Boyle	8	b Palmer	8
E. Greenwood l b w, b Palmer	3	st Jarvis, b Palmer	1
R. W. Hill c Slight, b Boyle	8	c Jarvis, b Boyle	16
E. O. Howis run out	0	b Palmer	3
Morton b Palmer	2	c Slight, b Boyle	6
Henty c Jarvis, b Palmer	5	c Jarvis, b Boyle	7
Mycroft not out	2	not out	0
Extras	25	Extras	12
Total	245	Total	176

Australian Eleven.

Murdoch, W. L. (Captain) run out	86	c Greenwood, b Mycroft	13
Alexander, G. b Mycroft	5		
Groube, T. U. c Henty, b Draper	1	b Mycroft	3
M'Donnell, P. S. b Mycroft	42	not out	12
Slight, J. b Mycroft	4		
Blackham, J. M. l b w, b Mycroft	1		
Bonnor, G. J. b Mycroft	27		
Palmer, G. E. b Morton	3		
Boyle, H. F. b Morton	13		
Moule, W. H. l b w, b Morton	0	not out	5
Jarvis, A. H. not out	0	st Henty, b Stratford	26
Extras	4	Extras	1
Total	186	Total	60

Umpires. Messrs. Lansdell and Brown.   Scorers, Mr. L. H. Elford and G. F. Salter.

Scorecard of Australians v Hastings 1880. Sussex County Cricket Club

In an article in the *Hastings and St Leonards Observer* in May 1880, mention is made of the many cricketers (including W G Grace) who regarded the ground at Hastings as 'the best and truest piece of turf in the

United Kingdom', and the writer said that 'the partial erection of a wall round the ground, and the planting of the banks with shrubs have greatly tended to relieve the ground of its former barren appearance, but there still remained one great eyesore'. This was 'the miserable, tumbled down shed – wretchedly deficient in accommodation of every kind – with visiting teams complaining bitterly.'

The Old Pavilion, built 1884. Barry Funnell

The New Pavilion, built 1935. Barry Funnell

At last by 1884 the Trustees had raised enough money towards the £1,000 needed to erect a new pavilion, which is the present building nestling under the wall of the gardens of the Devonshire Road houses. Here is a local report on the new building:

'The Committee of the Central Cricket and Recreation Ground have lately erected a new Pavilion at a cost exceeding £1,000. The building which is of an ornamental character, contains all the accommodation usually provided, as well as covered seats and a reserved enclosure.

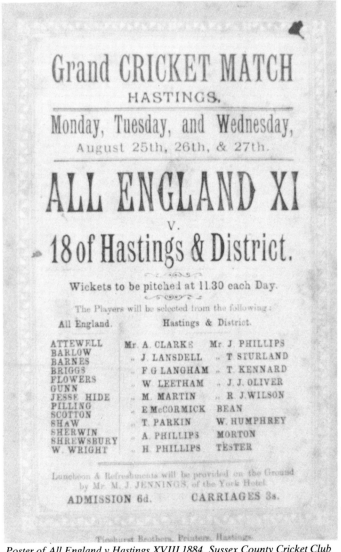

Poster of All England v Hastings XVIII 1884. Sussex County Cricket Club

'It has long been felt that such a building was required, and looking to the fact that for some years past the Committee has been urged to take this step, they now confidently appeal to the public for subscriptions towards raising the amount required.

'The ground is acknowledged to be one of the best in the Kingdom, and to fashionable towns like Hastings and St Leonards such a Pavilion is no doubt a necessity in order to compete with the neighbouring towns on the South Coast which offer many attractions of a similar character.'

Though the trustees would have preferred a larger building, Ground regulations said it must not be higher than the top of the 12ft wall behind it. It was a low building, 100ft long, in which 'the comfort of the players and others has been judiciously studied . . . as well as a long dining room, a dressing room fitted with washbasins, towel racks, etc, with lockers for placing cricket things in', also ' a useful room for the hanging of hats, coats etc . . . and there was a nice room for the ground keeper'. The pavilion had stained glass windows with a cricket motif. It remains a period piece, and was in full use until a new, more spacious successor was built in 1935 in the north-west corner of the ground.

The next occasion since the county game in 1880 in which the people of Hastings were privileged to see a top-class county side was in 1887 when on 28, 29, 30 July the full Yorkshire XI came down to play Eighteen of Hastings: they found powerful opposition, for the local side scored 380 against Yorkshire scores of 258 and 208-4. The hero was Herbert Pigg who scored as many as 180 against such England bowlers as Ulyett, Bates, Peel and Emmett. This must be one of the finest innings ever played on the ground. Unfortunately, the Club lost £15 18s on this enterprising venture and according to this account in *The Sporting Life* the trustees were understandably aggrieved by the lack of local support:

'To say that the executive of the Hastings Cricket Club are bitterly disappointed at the result of their efforts to give the Hastings and St Leonards inhabitants a sight of really first-class cricket would be to put their feelings into mild language indeed. They are utterly disgusted at the apathy exhibited by all of those from whom they might justly have hoped for help and sympathy. The shopkeepers, innkeepers and others who are those most benefitted by the action of the club are those most "backward" in coming "forward" and grudge even their small yearly subscription, let alone paying 6d a day to look at one of the best county elevens in England.'

There was plenty of correspondence, and it was pointed out that 90% of local people believed that the ground belonged to the Corporation – a belief that some have held right up to present times.

In spite of the financial failure of this county match, the Festival began in the same year, and must have done much to stimulate cricket in the district. By 1894 there was a problem of too many local clubs diluting the strength of a really representative Hastings team. This was the position: the Hastings and St Leonards Club was originally formed in 1861 as Hastings United and played on the East Hill. It had been formed after the dissolution of the East Sussex Club, which had been in action only since 1857 and played on the old racecourse at Bulverhythe. In 1874 the East Sussex Club was revived and lasted until 1880 when it provided the nucleus of the new South Saxons Club who played at Bopeep at the bottom of Filsham Road. In 1898 the Club started to play hockey in the winter, and the present South Saxons hockey club is well-known. We also read of the activities of the East End Club, still playing on the East Hill, and then there was also the Alexandra Club.

This diversity of clubs made fixture lists and team-raising hard to plan, especially if a man belonged to several clubs. At about the same time, plenty of outlying cricket was organised by the Big Houses such as: Crowhurst Park (the Papillons), Brickwall (Col Frewen), Broomham (the Ashburnhams), Windmill Hill (the Curteis family) and Baldslow Place (the Ebdens) – now Claremont School.

In 1894 the Hastings and St Leonards Club (reformed in 1873 after the creation of the Trust), and the Alexandra Club, both agreed to disband and then immediately to join forces into one new club, to be called the Hastings and St Leonards Club and Ground. The intention was to strengthen representative cricket, and this was assisted by the Corporation installing a water-pipe to the cricket square which enabled easier preparation of pitches. All these improvements persuaded the

Bomb craters on the ground July 1940. Trustees of the Central Ground

39

county cricket authorities to arrange the first ever county championship match here in 1895, and this eventually led to the creation of regular county cricket at Hastings. This seems a far cry from James Collier's first introduction of the game in 1745.

The coming to Hastings of annual big cricket meant that the trustees of the ground had to provide better seating and amenities. Before long, a permanent raised stand was put up at the South Terrace end, mainly for the use of county members. In the years between the wars W J Ransom acted as an admirable secretary.

The ground suffered damage in the war: in July 1940 some of the first bombs to fall on the United Kingdom fell on Hastings, including five on the Central Ground itself. Fortunately, they avoided the square; they were not very large bombs, but one made a 15 foot crater which was promptly investigated by the Hastings local historian, Barry Funnell, who went down on a ladder and noted the various lines of stratification so beloved by archaeologists. These lines went down out of sight towards the uncharted bottom of what was once a harbour. Within a very short time the hole was full of sea-water as a reminder of how low-lying the field is. It is said that after the raid the Germans claimed that they had successfully bombed Hastings Harbour. Presumably they were working on the out of date evidence of Kant's map of 1746.

When the RAF were stationed here, the great W R Hammond, as an officer, wished to requisition the ground totally for service use: the trustees opposed this, but were ready to make the ground available to the Services as much as possible, while some club cricket games continued as a boost to the morale of a virtually beleaguered town which was in a special zone from which most of the population had been evacuated.

After the war there was a considerable increase in the numbers of cricket-starved spectators, who flocked to the games and in 1949 the trustees issued a list of suggested improvements to the ground as well as a protest against the increased rates which the Council intended to impose. The proposals included:

1. The erection of show-cases on the Queen's Road frontage to be let to commercial firms.
2. New equipment to provide free seating for 500 on big occasions to save the cost of hire.
3. Improved sanitary arrangements.
4. Rebuilding the fire-damaged members' stand in concrete.
5. Terracing the Queen's Road covered stand in concrete giving shelter and a good view to some 1,000 people.
6. The eventual building of a magnificent pavilion and refreshment rooms near the public entrance at the top of Station Road.

Apart from the last one, all these improvements were duly carried out.

40

English Cup-tie: Hastings v Portsmouth 1908. David Padgham

The biggest undertaking concerned the area running alongside the Queen's Road. Originally there had been a roofed, slightly raised stand which spectators could use for such events as the football cup-tie between Hastings and Portsmouth in 1908. Later on came the show-cases, the shops, and above them the tiered seating known as the Alfred Coote Stand, opened in 1959. Over the topmost seats was a small pitched roof which recently has had to be removed since it had become unsafe and it was too costly to repair. Maintenance of any new structure produces further expense.

Another major improvement is the tower-shaped score-box built in alongside the old pavilion. Before that the only score-boards were those with flip-on numbers operated by boys: the board now no longer in existence near the Queen's Road entrance gate, was one of the originals. Between the members' stand and the new players' pavilion a building was put up in 1959, as score-box and committee rooms. This has, since 1978, been converted into a flat for the resident groundsman.

Another change was the suggestion by the committee in the autumn of 1964 that the ground should in future be known as 'Priory Meadow', echoing its original name of a hundred years ago. This re-naming has had some following, but the big board over the gates of the main entrance in Queen's Road still reads: 'The Central Cricket Ground'.

So much for ground improvements which helped to match the rising standard of cricket being played there, and not only by the visiting first-class cricketers. As mentioned earlier, there were several attempts in the

41

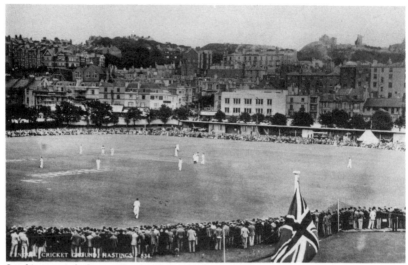

Looking towards Queens Road with the old stand c1938

View showing the Castle and the new stand of 1959. Author's Collection

past to create an ever stronger representative Hastings side by clubs amalgamating with each other. This was to happen yet again.

The Priory Club was started in 1939 as a Sunday-playing club, while others such as the Hastings and St Leonards Club, the East Sussex Club and the Ramblers, continued to use the ground on Saturdays. After much discussion, in 1957, the Hastings and St Leonards Club joined with the Priory to form one club, and this resulted in a top-class side containing some notable cricketers. Several of these have played for the Sussex

42

County 2nd Eleven; R H Thomson, played for Cambridge and Sussex in 1961-2, while Andy Morgan, a Hastings boy, won a Blue for Oxford University in 1969. In 1978 the Priory XI won the Sussex League

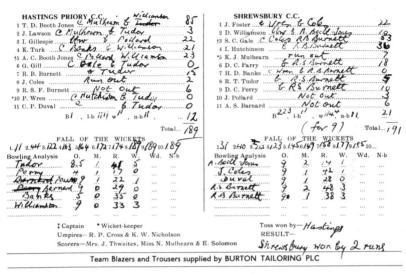

Scorecard of the Priory Club in Championship Final 1983. C Steggell

championship for the first time, and also won the area final of the Haig National Knock-out Competition, thus reaching the last 16 in all England. Five years later they were to excel themselves by reaching the final of the whole competition played at Lord's. It was a great disappointment to lose there to Shrewsbury by a mere three runs. The score-card is reproduced here to recall the players' names, and it is evident that a victory for the Priory seemed likely until a change of fortune at the very last moment. It was sad, but what a wonderful feat to have reached the final against such wide competition.

43

The Groundsmen

The success of a cricket club can be closely related to the skill of its groundsmen. Hastings has indeed been nobly served at the Central Ground. The first reference to 'a ground man' (sic) seems to be in 1887 when A T Manwaring is highly praised for the pitch he had prepared for the Festival. His successor was the famous Alf Tutt who is said to have reigned at the ground for fifty years. He was certainly in action in 1902 and continued into the 1940s. He was very protective about his field and anyone who dared to stray over the forbidden area was soon made aware of his error by a loud blare from Tutt on his megaphone.

Alf Tutt, Alf Dengate and Jim White – Groundsmen. Trustees of the Central Ground

He was succeeded in about 1947 by his son-in-law, Alf Dengate, of whom Alan Oakman and others have fond memories. Then came Harry Preston, a very good cricketer who had failed to establish himself in the very strong Kent county side just before the First World War. He sadly lost a hand in a mowing accident at Hastings. He was followed by W L (Len) Creese (1907-74). He was a South African who played for Hampshire between 1928-39. After his retirement he became coach at Sherborne school when David Sheppard was a boy there, and later he was appointed as groundsman at Hastings. He will be long remembered for his outstanding work on the field, his Alsatian dogs and his planting of decorative trees round the ground. He was a great character.

View across to South Terrace from top of Coote Stand 1988. Author's Collection

Creese was later lured away to the County Ground at Hove to improve the pitches there. The square at Hastings now developed serious trouble which led to the temporary suspension of county cricket here, so Creese came back and looked after the ground again. Mick Morley succeeded him and in 1978 the present groundsman, Jim Case, arrived.

Aerial view showing ground, about 1925. Trustees of the Central Ground

45

Record Attendance

Over the years there have been occasional references to 'Record Gates', but it would be difficult to say exactly which match has produced the greatest quantity of spectators or of money taken. The few references from Press reports include:

1893 The two festival games produced a record 16,500 spectators.

1932 Sussex v Kent: a final score-card printed on silk states: 'Record Breaking – over 20,000 attended the match.'

1948 Australians v South of England: *The Times* report: 'The oldest supporters of the festival say that never has there been such a multitude of spectators as there was to see the first day's play.'

1963 Sussex v Kent: 'There was a record gate of over £1,400 taken.'

It would be interesting to know which of the well-attended Sunday League matches has produced the best attendance total, which may well surpass the record for any single day's play in any first-class match played here.

View of north-east corner of the Ground c1910. Hastings Museum & Art Gallery

3 · County Cricket

There has been a brief reference to the first match of first-class status ever to be played on the new Central Ground. It was between Sussex and Kent on 4, 5, 6 September 1865. The counties had already met twice officially – with one win each – and this was a third contest privately arranged and regarded as 'the conquering match'. Thousands of people turned up to see the famous players, among whom were James and John Lillywhite, E Willsher, 'Farmer' Bennett, T Sewell and young Charlwood whose batting earned him a collection of £12. Thanks largely to poor time-keeping in the hours of play, the match was drawn. The spectators also had the chance of seeing the new over-arm bowling, legalised only in the previous year.

It was another fifteen years before the Sussex County authorities arranged an official county match at Hastings; it was against Leicestershire who had not so far won first-class status; but it was to be yet *another* fifteen years before the first-ever county championship match took place against Yorkshire in 1895. It had taken a long time for the Sussex County Club to realise the claims of Hastings as a venue, but from then on one match was allotted each year, increased to two in 1906, and within a year or so 'The County Week' became officially established. The delay had partly been because of the very low membership numbers from East Sussex. However, on the collapse of the Festival in 1909, Mr W E F Cheesman, who had succeeded William Carless as Secretary, persuaded the county authorities to consider Hastings more favourably, though the agreement for two matches annually was on condition that the county membership subscription for this area exceeded £200 per annum:

Since 1895 Sussex have played 135 championship matches here, with the tidy record of 46 wins, 44 losses, 43 draws, one tied match and one abandoned. It would be tedious to recall most of these, but there have been many memorable games, and a survey of those are given here. Every county has visited Hastings at least once, the most frequent visitors being Kent, with 47 appearances. Nearly every August the 'enemy' flooded over the nearby border, farmers in their finery, obvious 'Kentish' fans, and plenty of parsons. As young Sussex supporters we always eyed them all with barely disguised hostility.

Sussex v Surrey   14, 15, 16 July 1902

There was nothing in the previous encounters to suggest the possibility of the phenomenal high-scoring in this match. The scores were: Sussex 705-8 dec, and 170-4; Surrey 552, so in three days only 21 wickets fell for an aggregate of 1,427 runs, which was then a record match total for a first-class match in England. The Sussex score has never been surpassed as the record county total.

At the end of the first day Sussex were 419-6, with Ranji on 54*, made in 55 minutes. Next morning, being unable by law to declare until lunch on the second day, he decided to put on the pace, and was responsible for 180 runs out of the 286 added in 2½ hours before lunch at 1.30. In the last 70 minutes he enjoyed an unfinished stand of 160 for the ninth wicket with F W Tate 61*. For his 234* Ranji batted 205 minutes and hit 39 fours. This was the highest individual first-class score made at Hastings until beaten later by his nephew, K S Duleepsinhji, who scored 246 v Kent in 1929.

This remarkable innings reads as follows:

Mr C B Fry	c Brockwell, b Dowson	159
J Vine	c Dowson, b Richardson	92
E H Killick	lbw, b Clode	41
A E Relf	c & b Dowson	20
K S Ranjitsinhji	not out	234
Mr W Newham	c & b, Dowson	2
Mr G Brann	lbw, b Dowson	0
G Cox	c Hayes, b Clode	51
H R Butt	c Hayward, b Dowson	6
F W Tate	not out	61
C H G Bland	did not bat	
	B 25, lb 9, 5 nb	39
		705-8 dec

Fall of wickets: 238-1, 280-2, 331-3, 331-4, 334-5, 334-6, 526-7, 545-8.

Surrey bowling analysis: Lockwood 0-98, Richardson 1-143, Clode 2-129, Brockwell 0-99, Dowson 5-137, Jephson 0-30, Hayes 0-24.

In reply, Surrey's Abel 179 and Hayward 144, put on 246 for the first wicket, and then Abel and Capt H S Bush 122, added 197, so that when the second wicket fell with a Surrey score of 443, the first 10 wickets to fall in the match had produced as many as 1,148 runs. Surrey then 'collapsed' to be all out for 552.

Ranji (on right) plays his last game for Sussex 1920. Author's Collection

The bowlers had a miserable time, and it must all have seemed rather pointless. The pitch was perhaps made more favourable to batsmen as a result of the liberal application of Nottingham marl, a load being sent to Hastings every year. Ranji, inspite of his own success, disapproved of such treatment of the square as being bad for cricket.

This historic match was almost certainly celebrated in the doggerel verse of Albert Craig. Though based at the Oval, 'The Surrey Poet' would travel to other grounds successfully selling his topical cricket verses with their verbose titles all elegantly printed on coloured paper. He was a favourite everywhere. Craig was well aware of the verses' lack of literary merit and one of his best repartees came when a critic once said to him: 'Call yourself a poet? Huh! Why, I could write better poems myself!' Craig's courteous reply was: 'Doubtless, sir, Oh! doubtless – but could you *sell* them?'

Sussex v Yorkshire   28, 29, 30 August 1911

Another example of tall-scoring was Yorkshire's innings of 522-7 dec, of which George Hirst took the chance to make 218* out of 370 in only 210 minutes, with 3 sixes and 34 fours. Sussex could make no serious reply and lost by an innings, Vine alone showing any form with scores of 81 and 71.

Sussex v Surrey   1, 2, 3 September 1913

There was not always high scoring and in a close match Sussex had a good win by 21 runs. The home scores were 170 and 141 and Surrey led on the first innings with 195, of which Hobbs made 87. Yet they found the pitch increasingly difficult when they needed only 117 to win. W C (Razor) Smith of Surrey took 6-72 and 8-62 with his off-breaks, while George Cox, wheeling up his slow-medium left-handers, had figures of 6-54 and 4-22. On the Sussex side were P G H Fender and V W C Jupp, two young players who later had splendid careers with Surrey and Northants.

Sussex v Leicestershire   12, 14, 15 August 1922

On the opening day Leicester were all out for 148, A E R Gilligan clean bowling 6 batsmen for 45 runs with very fast deliveries; Leicester retaliated by capturing 8 Sussex wickets for 131. Next morning Maurice Tate 88, assisted by Gilligan, did much to take the score to 217, a useful lead. In Leicestershire's 2nd innings they were again harassed by Gilligan (5-55), but managed to reach a total of 245. This left Sussex 177 runs to win. Bowley with 52 stayed some time, but the batting steadily crumbled, and 63 were still wanted when Harold Gilligan came in last to join his brother. They stayed together for 41 runs, raising the Sussex hopes, until

Harold was 'ct and b' by Skelding, the Leicester fast bowler, who later became a famous umpire and cricket 'character'. In this game of ups and downs, one of the best finishes was seen – a margin of a mere 22 runs.

★

In 1923 as a very small boy I first attended the cricket week, and I have a very faint picture of gazing with awe at a rather rotund player walking past us on the field, and my father saying: 'Look, that's Richard Tyldesley, the Lancashire bowler!'

Sussex v Hampshire   6, 7, 8 August 1924

My recollections of this year are more distinct. I was sitting in our car next the Town Hall – you could park there in those days – when a ball landed on the roof of the Magistrate's court and bounced down on top of us. It was one of Tate's biggest swipes in his innings of 164, and from that moment I was completely hooked on cricket. Tate (as with many boys) became my hero, and this picture of him comes vividly to mind. To us, for many years, he was CRICKET – and all that it meant: 'As Tate went strolling to the wicket, wriggling his pads and holding his bat with the end cocked up, and shirt sleeves rolled well up over the elbow, there was a whiff of the village green about him. There were "good mornings" and pleasantries all round, but there was no doubt whatever about his intentions to hit the ball as hard and as often as possible. There never seemed any need to play himself in: if the first ball came right it would go for four. What entranced spectators about his batting was that he batted in the way they too would have chosen to bat. No frills, no fancies, and above all, plenty of fun for everyone. Few batsmen have more obviously enjoyed batting.'

Tate was always surrounded by small boys, and in the 1924 week there was a story going round about a ragged urchin who turned up at the gates with 6 half-pennies and 36 farthings which he had saved up to pay his entrance money of 1s. A bystander seeing this transaction insisted on paying for him and as a result 42 pieces of small change later ended up in the till of a sweet kiosk on the Ground.

★

By 1926 I was able to go to the matches by myself or with my friend Geoffrey Tree. We missed hardly a match for years. With sandwiches from home and swiss buns from Kings the Bakers of St Leonards, we caught the tram and arrived at the ground at about 10am to bag a seat on the raised part of the old football stand, alongside the Queen's Road.

Having staked our claim we would hurl tennis ball catches around. One day we turned up to find a vast woman sitting on OUR seat: this was an outrage, but after a time, possibly upset by the flying balls, she got up heavily and moved off. We pounced on our seat. We would peer at the players in their deck chairs, and occasionally seek autographs. My old book shows that in 1927 a young Etonian was playing for Sussex, called R C C Whittaker. He was a slow left-hander and on his debut he had the fine analysis of 5-36. He could not refrain, bless him, from writing '5 wickets' clearly after his signature.

Sussex v Notts   4, 5, 6 August 1926

On the opening day Notts lost their first 7 wickets for only 77, but thanks to Payton 110, they reached a total of 230. Bowley and Tate put on 56 for the 1st wicket, but a collapse followed and at the close the score was 116-6, and next morning young Larwood was again on the rampage. The novelist Dudley Carew, who described this match in his book *England Over*, claimed that Larwood 'is far and away the best bowler of any kind England has produced since the War.' I seem to remember stumps flying and almost every ball causing apprehension to slips as batsmen played and missed. Bowley with 94* batted through the innings, and Arthur Gilligan, with his 24 gave us a taste of things to come. So Notts had a lead of 24, and their second innings of 280 set Sussex a hard task. All I remember of this innings was the dismissal of A W Carr. He had scored 15, including a six off Tate, when he went all out for a big hit off one of Bowley's very slow leg-breaks. The ball appeared to be clearing the screen at the South

Tate and Gilligan in relaxed mood 1926. Author's Collection

Terrace end, when Tommy Cook, speeding round from the on-side (to quote Carew), 'jumped to the ball, got both hands to it, pushed it up in the manner of a goal-keeper, and caught it again with his right arm outstretched. . . . I have only to close my eyes to see again the almost comical look of anxiety upon Cook's face as he judged the flight of the ball before jumping for it.'

I too remember this, as well as the look of utter disbelief on Carr's face as he realised that he was out. Such moments of cricket are printed timelessly on the memory.

Sussex were faced with 305 to win and when 4 wickets went down for 55 (Larwood again), an easy win for Notts seemed likely. But Arthur Gilligan was in cavalier mood; in 80 minutes he scored 107 out of 152, with 3 sixes and 16 fours, mostly thumping great drives, punctuated with vain flashes at Larwood, who with the last ball before lunch shattered his stumps. I took a photo of the wrecked wicket.

To quote Carew again: 'As it turned out Sussex came within measurable distance of victory, and Arthur Gilligan played an innings which in the course of time will take on a rich and legendary hue.' There

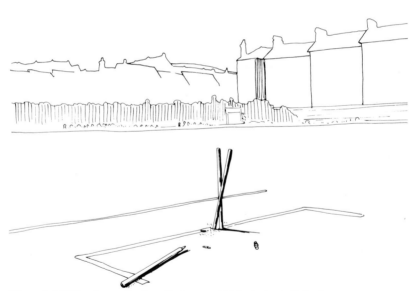

The end of Gilligan's great innings, 'b. Larwood 126'. Author's Collection

was nothing miraculous or sensational about it, but I can imagine schoolboys who were there that day grown into fathers and saying to their own boys after witnessing some heroic display of batting: 'Ah, but you should have seen Gilligan's hundred at Hastings back in 1926.' I was indeed one of those schoolboys.

52

The Sussex XI of 1931 – 4th in Championship. Trustees of the Central Ground

Sussex v Kent   7, 9, 10 August 1926

The very next day on 7 August, Arthur Gilligan did it again with a similar dashing innings of 126 in 2 hours, with 4 sixes and 14 fours, and he coped just as well with the sinuous wiles of Freeman and Marriott as he had with the sheer speed of Larwood. In spite of a typical Woolley score of 104, Kent were 118 behind on the first innings, and then Sussex made 284-8 dec, with Cook 100*. The problem was how to get Kent out in the four hours that remained. In the end, Tate's bowling made victory certain with 5 more wickets to add to the 6 of his first innings, and as he also scored 73 and 11, he showed his usual Hastings form. Woolley was again top scorer with 45, but it was Gilligan who made the match memorable. On the second morning play was delayed for 40 minutes by a sea-fret, one of the hazards of a sea-side ground, which always causes an especially maddening delay.

It was most unusual to have three matches in succession at Hastings, but this year Leicester was added to the week. To my disappointment I was unable to be there, but perhaps it was just as well, because on the third day Sussex dropped as many as 8 catches, 7 of them from E W Dawson, whose frequent lives enabled him to score 118. It must have

53

been agony to see the usually so brilliant home side field so appallingly, but it did not cost them the match, which was drawn. On the last day K S Duleepsinhji scored 73* with real promise of great moments to come.

Sussex v Notts   10, 11, 12 August 1927

This match was very like the game of the previous year. Sussex needed 308 to win and failed in the last few overs, being all out for 279. When the 8th wicket fell at 217, the end seemed near, but Arthur Gilligan threatened once again to turn the tables. He made a brilliant 66*, but his partners failed him, being dismissed by a tall, young, slow left-hander named Voce. He bowled then in very different style from his later vicious bouncing inswingers.

Sussex v Essex   14, 16, 17 July 1928

As in 1926 there were three county matches. The first was in mid-July, and I remember it well because, after luckily winning a scholarship, my Headmaster at Hydneye House, E G Maltby, later to be connected with the Festival, asked me how I would like to celebrate it. There was only one answer to that – a request for a visit to Hastings for the county cricket. We all sat on benches at the South Terrace end, fortified by tea provided by my parents. My chief recollection was seeing a young Sussex batsman, George Pearce, who in his innings of 36*, smote a ball from J W H T Douglas right out of the ground into Station Road. Tate, as usual, obliged with scores of 126 and 62, as well as taking 6 wickets. 16 July 1928 was for me a most memorable outing.

Sussex v Notts   8, 9, 10 August 1928

A few weeks later I was back on my usual bench again watching Sussex lose by 2 wickets in yet another close game with Notts. Notts needed 187 to win, and when 5 wickets were gone for 98 Sussex hopes ran high, but W Payton, a tough old campaigner, scored 57* and with Larwood 16* saw Notts home. Larwood also took 11 wickets. I suppose we were lucky to see so much of this great bowler in his early days, but I doubt if the Sussex players enjoyed it. In this game Tate twice clean bowled George Gunn; in the course of 9 meetings between May 1928 and September 1929 Tate clean bowled this genius of a batsman no less than 6 times.

Sussex v Kent   11, 13, 14 August 1928

This match produced too many runs to allow a finish, but in their first innings Sussex managed to reach a total of 405, after losing the first 7 wickets for a mere 105 – a wonderful recovery. Young Harry Parks made 158* and had a stand with Arthur Gilligan, who made a chanceless 104 runs in 95 minutes. He kept on saving Sussex at Hastings so it is no wonder it was his favourite ground. Little Tich Cornford also batted neatly to score 57. Kent topped the Sussex total with hundreds from Woolley 120 and J L Bryan 109: later Duleep made 107 and Bowley 92 – all attractive innings. In the last moments of the game Leslie Ames took his 103rd victim of the season as wicket-keeper and so beat Huish's previous record. I remember the anxious appeals ending at last in Ames's triumph.

Sussex v Kent 10, 12, 13 August 1929

There can have been few more courteous or kindly men than K S Duleepsinhji, but on 20 July 1929 he was hopping mad. In a long spell of hot dry weather Gilligan had not inspected the pitch before deciding to bat first at Maidstone. He was horrified to find out later that the pitch had been heavily watered; Freeman made the most of it, took 7-16; Sussex were all out for 69 and lost the match by an innings. On the way back from Maidstone Duleep had said to Gilligan, with quiet, but very firm precision – 'Arthur, I promise you that when we play Kent at Hastings next month I will make 100 in each innings, *and I mean it.*'

K S Duleepsinhji, hero of 1929. Trustees of the Central Ground

On 10 August, Sussex won the toss on a perfect wicket, and at lunch time, after two hours batting, the score was an astonishing 201-4. Yes! 201 runs before lunch. Bowley went early. Then Duleep joined Harold Gilligan and they put on 121 runs in 66 minutes before Gilligan was caught in the deep. In the very last over before lunch, Duleep, having scored 115 in 100 minutes, was caught at mid-on off C S Marriott's first ball. He was very sick with himself for getting out. He thought: 'Uncle always told me that when I make 100 I must then concentrate on getting 200, and when I reach a double-century, I must take fresh guard. Anyway, wait till my next knock, and I'll do what he advised.' This was the real Bradman approach, and Ranji did in fact make many double-centuries.

Kent replied to the Sussex score of 428 with 398, of which C H Knott made a dashing 140*, and at close of play on the second day the Sussex score read:

Bowley	lbw Freeman	30
A H H Gilligan	c Ashdown, b Wright	4
K S Duleepsinhji	not out	149
R L Holdsworth	lbw Marriott	8
Jas Langridge	not out	18
	extras	6
		215-3 wickets

Duleep had reached 100* out of 132 in 90 minutes, and his 149* had taken only two hours. Next morning we were all ready for more: there had been a record attendance of 8,000 on the second day and we were not to be disappointed. Duleep took a single off the first ball and then went on to hit Freeman hard and high. To quote H S Altham: 'He tore him to shreds.' One ball he was halfway down the wicket to drive, to the next he was leaning into a sweet late-cut, or a delicate glance. On reaching the double-century he had fully intended to make, he opened up with some huge drives. He hit Freeman for two consecutive sixes, one of which went through a window of the Prince's Hotel at the west end of South Terrace, and he was going for a third six when he was brilliantly caught by a substitute fielding on the very edge of the boundary in front of the Members' stand. He had scored 246 out of 351 in 195 minutes, chiefly by means of 5 sixes and 31 fours. He had not only achieved two hundreds in the match as he had promised, but his score of 246 beat his uncle's previous highest score for the ground. As a supplement to a match total of 361, Duleep snapped up 6 catches in the slips, 5 of them off Tate.

Apart from Duleep's performance the game was memorable for producing no fewer than 1,451 runs for the loss of 36 wickets – still the second highest aggregate for a county match. The hitting went on to the very end. When Kent wanted 404 to win they were all out for 244, with

56

	BATSMEN	RUNS	HOW OUT	BOWLER	TOTAL
1	Bowley E H	3 1 1 1 4 1 1 1 2 1 4 2 2 1 1 3 /	L B W	Freeman	30
2	Gilligan Mr AH	4 /	Ct Ashdown	Wright	4
3	Duleepsinhji K	1 1 1 4 1 1 2 1 2 1 4 4 2 4 4 1 4 1 2 1 1 1 2 1 1 1 1 1 1 / 4 2 2 1 1 4 4 4 4 4 4 3 1 6 2 2 4 4 1 1 1 4 / 1 1 1 1 1 1 1 1 /	Ct Sub	Freeman	246
4	Holdsworth Mr RL		L B W	Marriott	8
5	Langridge Jas	3 1 1 4 1 1 2 1 1 1 4 2 1 1 1 1 2 /	Ct Ames	Ashdown	32
6	Wensley AF	1 1 1 4 1 2 1 4 4 1 1 2 4 4 4 1 /	Ct Ashdown	Freeman	33
7	Grimston Mr gs	1 1 1 2 1 /	Bowled	Marriott	6
8	Cornford W.	1 2 2 /	Not	Out	6
9	Tate M W	4 1 4 /	Bowled	Marriott	9
10	Hollingdale RA		} DID NOT BAT		–
11	Cook T E				–
	WIDES				-
	BYES	2 2 1			5
	LEG BYES	1 1			2
	NO BALLS				-

| 1 1 1 1 | 1 1 1 4 1 2 4 1 1 1 4 1 1 1 1 | 1 1 4 6 1 6 6 // for 9 TOTAL | 381 |

Duleep's historic 246 – scored by the author aged 12. Author's Collection

Ames scoring 121. Tate, inspite of the high-scoring, took 13 wickets in the match, with analyses of 6-126 and 7-58, which he regarded as being one of his best-ever bowling feats.

Another historic feature of this game was a collection made for the benefit of Frank Woolley of Kent. This was believed to be the first time a collection had been made on any ground, for a player belonging to another county. He was one of those whom Sussex were always relieved to see dismissed, but at the same time there was a touch of regret that such graceful and effortless batting should come to an end. There has never been another Woolley.

Sussex v Glamorgan   7, 8, 9 August 1935

Here was one of the most exciting finishes ever seen at Hastings. Glamorgan needed 165 runs to win in 105 minutes; Sussex, though weakened by the absence of bowlers Jim Cornford and G Pearce, seemed to have a grip on the game until G Laver, with 65* saw them through to victory off the fourth ball of the last over. This three-wicket win had been made possible by a remarkable innings by Cyril Smart. In reply to the Sussex score of 289, Glamorgan had lost 5 wickets cheaply before Smart joined his captain Maurice Turnbull. When the innings was over for 384, Smart was left not out, having scored 151 in three hours with 6 sixes and 16 fours. I remember one buffet pitching far into the garden of one of the houses in Devonshire Road.

57

Sussex v Glamorgan   4, 5, 6 August 1937

Glamorgan repeated the 1935 victory by scoring 190 for 7 wickets. This time it was not thanks to Smart (who made 0 and 13), but to Austin Matthews who, bowling in great heat, had the fine analyses of 7-75 and 7-57 in the Sussex scores of 384-9 dec and 163.

All was even going up to half way, but the Sussex second innings failed except for the top score of 36 by Robert Stainton, the schoolmaster from Battle. Dyson and E Davies opened the final Glamorgan innings with a stand of 94, but though wickets then began to fall, Glamorgan had the final word. In his first innings, J C Clay hit 24 runs off an over from Jas Langridge, bombarding the Members' stand lustily.

Sussex v Kent   7, 9, 10 August 1937

The second game of the week was won comfortably by Sussex and was memorable for the dramatic return to the side of Maurice Tate. At the start of the season the Sussex Committee had announced that they intended to rest Tate (now aged 42) in some early away games. Tate did not like this at all and said that he never felt fitter. On 26 June he hurt himself and when he recovered he found it difficult to regain his place in a side which was at the time doing so well. It seemed that Tate had come to the end of the road and he rather unwisely expressed his disappointment in the Press. On 3 August the Committee announced that they were not re-engaging him for 1938. But suddenly, just when it seemed that the Hastings crowd would never again see their hero, Tate was informed on the Friday evening that he was to play against Kent the next day.

Sussex won the toss and when Tate came in to bat at 5.38pm, with the healthy total of 413-8 on the board, he was greeted by as big a welcome as the ground had ever known. His many friends prayed that he would succeed, and after a careful start he did not fail them. He made a faultless 73 out of the 139 runs added in 67 minutes, only to be brilliantly caught on the boundary by Tom Spencer, the one-time Hastings cricketer. Next day the papers were ecstatic:

TATE'S ANSWER TO THE SELECTORS
KENT BOWLING FLOGGED AT HASTINGS
SUNSHINE SIXES BRING JOY TO FESTIVAL CROWD

and that was not the end of it, because he also took 6 good wickets. In spite of this glorious come-back, Tate was not to be re-engaged. However, in April 1939 he returned to his favourite Hastings ground to do some coaching, and I was privileged to take part. How wonderful it was to bat to the bowling of the man who had so long been our hero, and many years later in 1976 I had the pleasure of writing Tate's biography.

58

Sussex v Northants   3, 4, 5 August 1938
Sussex v Kent   6, 8, 9 August 1938

This week provided two easy wins for Sussex, chiefly because of two fine innings by Hugh Bartlett, who scored 114 against each visiting team. In the first game against Northants, he came in when Sussex had lost 5 cheap wickets, opened up carefully, and finally hit 3 sixes and 14 fours. Against Kent he came in in a similar situation and then hit 2 sixes and 12 fours, coping very well with the fine bowling of D V P Wright, who took 7-113 in the Sussex total of 447-9 dec. One of Bartlett's hits off Wright went through a window in South Terrace.

Throughout 1938 Bartlett produced some big-hitting performances worthy of Jessop. He scored 175 against the Players at Lord's, and ended the season with a score of 157 in two hours for Sussex against the Australians at Hove. He was a tall left-hander with great power, but seemed a terribly tentative starter. In his opening over he was almost incapable of moving his bat, but when he had at last made good contact with the ball and hit a boundary, all was well. Beautiful, clean, very long hits, and cracking square cuts. I was lucky enough to see him score a century in the first three innings I saw him bat. The 1938 Hastings week was Bartlett week, long to be recalled by all who witnessed these two centuries.

Sussex v Kent – a record crowd in 1947. Trustees of the Central Ground

Now that we have been back to the 1930s we can consider what changes can be seen from cricket of some 40 years ago. First, the players themselves: there were fewer tall giants in those days – Alan Oakman was an exception – and we saw far more elderly, rather rotund gentlemen who would have found the flash fielding of the modern one-day game impossible to emulate. Beards were rare: it was really the 1970s which produced teams resembling the group photos of a hundred years ago. The fashion now seems to be fading, as also the vogue for long hair.

59

Cricketing attire shows many differences. In those days flannels really were flannel, both trousers and shirts: none of the twill or polyester trousers seen today, and certainly no T-shirts with cut-off sleeves, and no advertising either on clothes or on the boards fringing the ground. Some amateurs, following Ranji's example, wore fluttering silk shirts, and others, such as D R Jardine and E R T Holmes, wore a sort of cravat and had their shirt-sleeves rolled elegantly just below the elbow. Anything resembling a track-suit would have been quite unacceptable, even for practice at the nets. There would be no sweat-bands for head or wrist and caps and blazers were the rule, county ones or gaily-coloured Oxbridge Blues, Harlequins, Free Foresters, Quidnuncs or I Zingari. Many preferred to go bare-headed even when batting. Floppy hats such as seen today (often fallen to the ground) did not exist, but Jack Holmes, of Sussex, sometimes wore a hat and so did R A Young, who actually kept wicket in glasses.

There was no sign of special head protection until Hendren's half-jokey 3-peaked cap was worn as a defence against the West Indies' fast bowlers in 1933. No similar one was seen until Brearley and Amiss set a new example. It was not uncommon for a player to wear a dark sash round his middle. On the feet were good solid, heavily studded boots, kept clean. Rubber soles and ordinary shoes were never considered, though I remember J G W Davies wore tennis shoes when fielding in the deep on a dry day. Batting gloves were far less bulky, but no less efficient.

What about on the field of play? No batsman ever stood facing the bowler with his bat poised in the air and few had bats heavier than 2lb 3oz. No player ever came to the wicket swinging his bat in a circle. I believe that Tony Greig was the originator of both these fashions. We never saw bowlers prefacing their spell of bowling by stealthily bowling a practice ball to a fielder as a loosener. There was no excessive display of congratulation at a fallen wicket, and none of this single-hand slapping.

Before the game began a few players might come out on to the field, without pads, and play a few balls, sometimes to the danger of the public crowding round them. There was no show of physical exercises, or running circuits of the ground. Imagine W G Grace indulging in press-ups before the game! Since there were no loud-speakers, announcements were made by boys coming round the ground holding up a blackboard, eg 'Sussex won the toss and will bat'. The scoreboards were often unsophisticated affairs with flip-on numbers worked by boys with varying efficiency. No flash light to identify a fielder. The scorers still dealt in minutes in timing the length of a batsman's innings rather than in the number of balls he received.

Up to the middle of the 1920s the roller might still be drawn by a horse wearing heavy oversize goloshes. Scorecards were brought round very frequently instead of men selling lottery tickets. Sometimes a boy would

60

come along selling tea-tickets at 1s 6d, which enabled one to partake of a dainty tea in an enclosure, served by waitresses in neat black and white dresses. Much of the seating was on hard benches, planks balanced precariously on crude stumps; no wonder there was need for that strange old character, wearing a single spectacle over one eye, who used to sell cushions, 'three-pennyworth of comfort – kept the splinters out of your bum'. Then there were the boys who dashed out with telegrams on to the field. Was it an invitation to play for England – the birth of a child – or just the winner of the 3.30? We used to admire the restraint of those players who just stuffed the telegram into a pocket – unopened. Ah, well! 'Tempora mutantur' etc.

Post War Cricket

Sussex v Surrey   9, 10, 11 August 1950

This was one of those all too frequent matches which Sussex ought to have won, but did not. Against the home side's scores of 404-7 dec and 150-5 dec, Surrey, with 257, managed to save the follow-on by a mere 3 runs. After what seemed a safe declaration by James Langridge, Surrey were left with 298 to win in 170 minutes. They made a poor start, but J F Parker made 87 in 63 minutes with 2 sixes and 12 fours and later A V Bedser, with 57 in 50 minutes, continued to go for the runs. Two skied catches were dropped, and Surrey got home with 20 minutes and 3 wickets to spare. On the opening day John Langridge 70 and David Sheppard 129, put up 149 runs for the first wicket and nothing seemed less likely than a Sussex defeat, but there it was, they let the game slip, and lost.

Sussex v Kent   26, 28, 29 July 1952

Two years later a similar match, this time went the way of Sussex. On the opening day Kent scored a satisfactory 302, two left-handers, Ufton 119* and B R Edrich 82, taking the honours. Sussex replied with 172, but then got back into the game by dismissing Kent for 174 (Oakman 4-30). Sussex were left with 305 to win, which seemed too many, but John Langridge 105 and David Sheppard 140 gave a heartening start with 216 for the first wicket in 3 hours: this put victory in sight and Sussex got home by 7 wickets.

Sussex v Yorkshire   22, 23, 24 July 1953

This year Sussex were leading in the championship for the first time since 1932 and David Sheppard, now captain, played his highest innings in Hastings matches. After dismissing Yorkshire for 226, Sussex replied with 387-3 dec, thanks to a stand of 279 between Sheppard and George Cox, who made 144 of these runs. Sheppard was left with 181*, which included 3 sixes and 20 fours. Two of the sixes came off consecutive balls from Halliday. What a feast of batting these two glorious batsmen produced.

Sussex County Cricket XI 1953 (2nd in Championship)
(back row) R T Webb, J M Parks, A S Oakman, D L Bates, A E James, K G Suttle
(sitting) G Cox, James Langridge, D S Sheppard (capt), Jn Langridge, D J Wood

The Sussex XI of 1953 – runners-up in Championship. Sussex County Cricket Club

Sussex v Kent   25, 27, 28 July 1953

In the second match of the week George Cox went one better with a score of 145, thus joining the select group of those who had scored a century in each match of the week, namely Arthur Gilligan, V W C Jupp, J H Parks, John Langridge and H T Bartlett.

Cox in full flow was one of the most exciting batsmen in the world, and no player aroused in me such expectations, sometimes however shattered because he tended to be out for 0 more often than other great batsmen. It was the price we had to pay for all his other wonderful innings. I can still see (and hear) that unique half-cut, half-drive that sent the ball whistling past cover. What a joyful personality.

Sussex v Notts   10, 12, 13 July 1954

This was another game that Sussex lost after twice declaring at 350-8 dec and 198-7 dec. There were good scores from Jim Parks 135, Cox 58 and 77 and Sheppard 68. In spite of an elegant 120 from Hardstaff, Notts were all out for 286 with Ian Thomson, who often bowled well at Hastings, taking 6 wickets. Notts had to make 263 to win in only 165 minutes, but they got them for the loss of 6 wickets, with only 3 balls to go in the last over – a most frantic finish. Their heroes were Giles 89 and Stocks 77*. They put on 143 runs in only 70 minutes: Sussex should surely have held the game tighter.

Sussex v Kent   21, 22, 23 July 1965

In one of the rare games in which a double declaration ended in a win, Sussex 295-8 dec and 99-6 dec, were able to force a victory against their old rivals, who with scores of 211 and 159 lost by 24 runs, the last man going down when Leary was caught at the wicket off Cooper from the fourth ball of the last over. It was all very tense. Suttle made 112 and the young Nawab of Pataudi 78 in their very different styles. They had steered Sussex towards a good score, and Kent found the bowling of Thomson difficult, only R C Wilson with 72 and 50 having much success.

Sussex v Kent   20, 21, 22 July 1968

This was Dexter's match. 20 July 1968 was a day to savour. He was playing in his first championship game for two years, and as he relates in a later chapter, there was a chance of a recall to the England team. When Sussex batted first, Buss and Suttle were out for 6 runs, and Dexter at No 5 was rushed into immediate action. Before long the score was 27-4, and later 85-5, but in his first match as Sussex skipper Mike Griffith gave good support: Dexter had reached the nineties when a shower held up play, and tea was taken with his score at 99*. His century was reached in 3 hours and 4 minutes.

He now opened up in his most majestic manner, and at 6.20 he was on 180*: he believed that play was to end at 6.30 (though in fact it was to go on until 7.00) so he went all out to try to reach 200 in the next ten minutes. In one over from Dixon he hit 6-4-6-4-3, thus reaching his 200, but in the next over he was well caught at extra-cover off a ball from Underwood, who in the course of the day most unusually conceded as many as 144 runs. Dexter's 203 was made out of 313 in 5 hours with 3 sixes (one on the Town Hall) and 23 fours. One can still hear the gun-shot crack of the ball as it left Dexter's bat – a unique sound special only to him. This was his highest score for Sussex.

I had hopefully taken a party of boys from my school, Hydneye House, to see some county cricket, always a bit of a gamble. What a treat we had to witness one of the most talked-about innings ever seen at Hastings. As the *Hastings & St Leonards Observer* commented: 'If such a knock could be guaranteed just half a dozen times a season, the future of county cricket would be assured.'

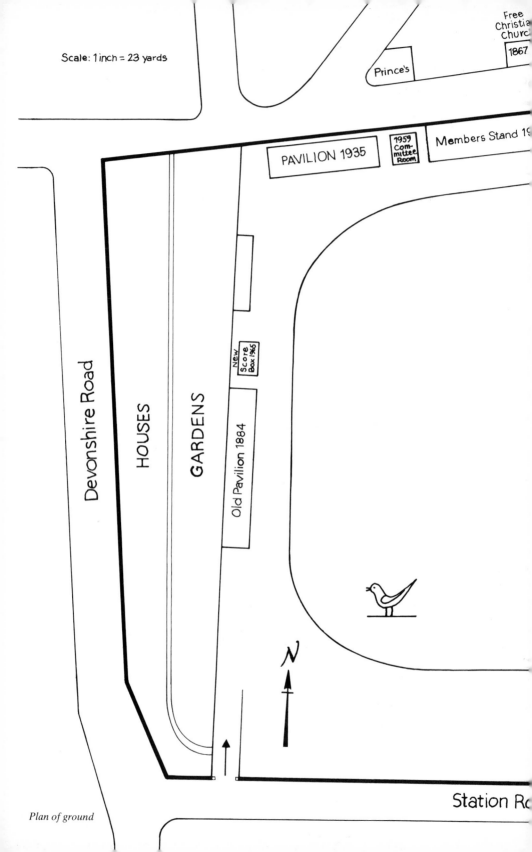

Scale: 1 inch = 23 yards

Free
Christia
Churc
1867

Prince's

PAVILION 1935

1959 Committee Room

Members Stand 19

Devonshire Road

HOUSES

GARDENS

New Score Box 1965

Old Pavilion 1884

N

Station R

Plan of ground

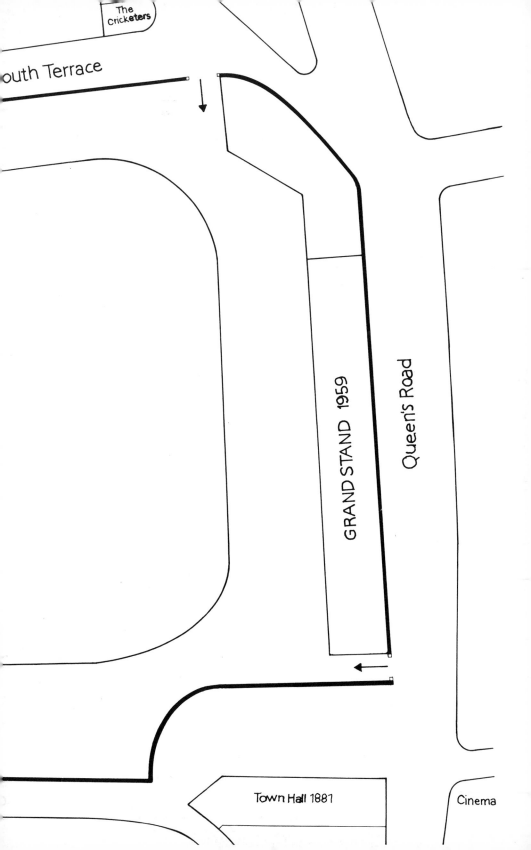

The Cricketers

outh Terrace

GRAND STAND 1959

Queen's Road

Town Hall 1881

Cinema

In July 1969 after the match against Glamorgan, Mike Griffith the Sussex captain reported the Hastings pitch as being unfit for County cricket, though the scores of Sussex 180 and 228 and Glamorgan 276 and 204-6 dec do not suggest any great problem. In the following county match in August the scores still seemed reasonable, and they included a fine innings of 169 by Luckhurst of Kent: after the complaint however the county authorities did not even wait for an official pitch inspection and ruling, but instantly cancelled county cricket at Hastings for 1970 – a sad blow for all local supporters.

Len Creese who had done such marvellous work on the Central Ground until he was lured away to Hove to improve things there, now came back as consultant to assist the new groundsman to correct the deficiencies of the pitch caused partly by clover growth.

In 1972 the Sussex County committee lifted the ban on the pitch and arranged a single game with Kent, but since then there has never been more than one first-class match a season. In fact, between 1976 and 1979 and in 1983, there was no county match at all; this was probably the result of a deliberate policy to concentrate more county games at Hove.

Sussex v Kent   2, 3, 4 May 1973

One famous bowler seemed to relish the Hastings pitch, and if conditions were at all helpful there was no one more 'deadly' than Derek Underwood. In 1964 when the wicket became dusty he took 9-28 in a Sussex innings of 155. Three years later – now on a rain-affected pitch – he had 14 victims (7-38 and 7-44), and in their second innings the last 6 Sussex wickets collapsed for a mere 10 runs.

In 1973 he struck again. On the opening day Kent scored 282-5 and declared. Next day a wet morning gave way to sunshine, and Sussex were shot out for 67, Underwood taking 5-43. Heavy thunderstorms followed, and the final morning found the ground almost under water. However the Kent team, anxious to start play and force a win, waded about bare-footed with mops doing all they could to assist the groundsmen and fire-brigade. The Sussex team looked on at all this combined activity, and regarded the Kent efforts as somewhat over zealous, almost unseemly. By a miracle, play was possible by 4 o'clock, and the sun was shining brightly as the Sussex batsmen started on their second innings with every intention of saving the game as there was not much time left for play. But Underwood revelled in conditions which might have been made for him. In 20 overs and one ball, the game was over, Sussex skittled out for 54 which equalled the score made by Kent in the previous year, when it became the lowest innings total ever made at Hastings. Underwood's bowling analysis was:

10.1-6-9-8

Only three bowlers, Laker (8-1 in 1950), Shackleton (8-4 in 1956), and Peel (8-5 in 1883) had conceded fewer runs in an innings in which 8 wickets were taken. Greig must have felt most disappointed at what happened in what was his first championship match as captain of Sussex. We shall hear more of an Underwood performance in a match of 12 years later.

Looking towards South Terrace and the Chapel targets c1975. Author's Collection

Sussex v Warwickshire 31 May, 2, 3, June 1975

The last match before county cricket ended temporarily at Hastings was a very strange one. Sussex made 370-8 dec and 219-6 dec but lost most unexpectedly to Warwickshire with scores of 235 and 355-2. On the opening day Sussex were 24-3 when Greig came in: in the next 4¼ hours he hit 226 with 6 sixes and 18 fours. Four of the sixes came off consecutive balls. It was a chanceless innings, the fourth highest ever made at Hastings, and it enabled Sussex to declare after 100 overs. Warwickshire were then dismissed for 235 (Greig 3-77), and Sussex, batting again, made a quick 219-6 declared, Greig again excelling with 71. Few believed that Warwickshire could score as many as the 355 needed for victory, but this was reached for the loss of only 2 wickets in 4¼ hours. Amiss and John Jameson put on 188 for the first wicket before Jameson was out for 112, Kallicharan was run out at 225 for 2, and then Kanhai 57* and Amiss 143* easily knocked off the runs. This was a terrible disappointment for Sussex, but the game will be better remembered as a personal triumph for Greig. On the Sunday there was a League match also against Warwickshire, and in this Greig scored a rapid 108*. so in the two matches over three days he actually scored 405 runs, including 12 sixes. What fun for the spectators.

Sussex v Kent   30 June, 1, 2, July 1984

The only first-class match at Hastings to end in a tie was full of surprises from beginning to end. On the opening day 21 wickets fell for 257 runs, with Kent all out for 92 (C M Wells 5-25), and Sussex doing not much better with a score of 143 (C M Wells 51). In Kent's second innings Derek Underwood had gone in third as night watchman, and next day, while Kent wickets tumbled – they were 110-7 at one time – Underwood stuck it out valiantly. At 155-8 the Australian bowler Alderman joined Underwood, and these two put on 53 for the 8th wicket, until Underwood was at long last LBW to Reeves for 111 at 208-9. This was his 618th innings in first class cricket in a career of 22 years, and his previous top score was 80 (scored in 1969): he had no other score reaching fifty.

As his innings went on and on the Sussex supporters naturally wanted to see him out, but at the same time they liked to think of this popular old 'enemy' achieving a first hundred. It was an absurd situation. He was missed in the slips in the nineties – almost it seemed on purpose – but when he was at last out Sussex were still well placed with Kent only 157 runs on. They now made the big mistake of allowing Alderman not only to score 52* – his highest score ever, but to put on 35 more runs for the last wicket with Jarvis, a well-known rabbit. For Sussex to allow two non-batsmen to reach their highest scores in the same innings was a terrible lapse. So Kent was able to reach 243, but Sussex however needed 'only' 193 to win. After a bad start at 89-5, at lunch time the score was 186-6, and all seemed well. I remember going off to lunch with my wife confident that a few more minutes would see Sussex safely through. On resuming however it immediately became 186-7, 190-8, and 190-9: the scores became levelled at 192 when poor young Smith the substitute wicket-keeper gave another slip catch to Tavare, and the game was tied. The batting after lunch reminded me of a prep school match with frenzied running and unnecessary swiping – in fact sheer panic. But what a match to remember!

Sussex v Lancashire   30 June, 1, 2, July 1985

On the opening day Sussex scored 310-6 d: Mendis made 103, Imran Khan 70, C M Wells 69*, and there was a cameo gem of an innings of 40 by Ian Greig. Patterson, the West Indian, was being tried out for Lancashire this season, and Greig hooked his fast vicious bouncers superbly. In reply Lancashire were all out for 173, losing the last 5 wickets for 13 runs: Imran clean bowled three batsmen for 0 each in 14 balls after being warned by umpire Whitehead for short-pitched bowling. When in their second innings Sussex scored 193-0, all seemed set fair for victory: Green made 78* and Mendis completed his second hundred of the match off the last ball of the day. Only two others, J T Tyldesley and K S Duleepsinhji, had previously made two hundreds in a match at Hastings.

Barclay declared overnight leaving Lancashire 331 to win off 105 overs: they started disastrously, losing 5 wickets for 60, but then Jack Simmons, aged 44, showed all his experience in rallying the side, and the score rose to 207 before the 7th wicket fell. Time was running out with Lancashire now hoping to draw the game, but Barclay, who so far during the season had bowled only 11 overs in Championship matches, went on wheeling away with his off-breaks for 30 overs and took 5 wickets: when he also brilliantly caught Simmons at slip the game was won. Simmons had made an excellent 101 in 168 minutes, and nearly saved his side. I enjoyed this game enormously, and not simply because Sussex had won: that final afternoon's slanting sunlight made the ground look even more romantic than usual.

Sussex v Northants   29, 30 June, 1 July 1986

This was yet another of those games in which Sussex declared twice – and lost the match. Sussex scored 283-9 d and 173-3 d while Northants' first innings was only 136, thus missing the follow-on figure by only 2 runs. The last day began with Northants needing 321 to win, and when Larkin and Boyd-Moss were each out for 0, and the total was 1-2, Sussex were full of hope . . . and the hard wicket was starting to crumble. But Lamb was on the warpath: he had just heard that he had been dropped from the England team owing to loss of form, but his retort was a magnificent innings of 157 made off only 153 balls in 185 minutes. He put on 172 for the 3rd wicket with Capel 54, and Bailey made 57.

I had to leave the ground just before Lamb was out, and I felt that I had seldom seen a greater innings, with 27 boundaries streaking in all directions. When Lamb was at last caught, Sussex took fresh heart, and the pendulum had swung. At the tea interval Northants needed 33 to win with 2 wickets left. When thet 9th man was out at 301, Walker joined Mallender, and they still needed 20 runs. Imran Khan came on again, but he seemed to be trying too hard, the runs kept coming, and after 6 singles in a row, Walker drove Imran for a 7th one, and the game was won. Sussex had at several stages looked likely winners, but yet again had been unable to clinch the victory. It was a bitter disappointment, but it was one of the most exciting matches ever seen at Hastings.

In 1987 for the first time ever in a first-class match at Hastings not a single ball could be bowled throughout three days of persistent rain, and this Sussex v Yorkshire match was abandoned.

Sussex v Kent   2, 3, 4 July 1988

Supporters therefore looked forward to this match even more eagerly than usual. Alas for Sussex, they were skittled out before lunch for a miserable score of 71, and Kent replied with 288 – an enormous lead. When Sussex went in again they batted more resolutely, but with a close-of-play total of 122-3 they still needed 95 runs to avoid an innings defeat. Paul Parker, the Sussex captain, who was 31* overnight, was determined to stay in and set Kent a tough target. Curbing his usual attacking strokes and assisted by Martin Speight, who made his first county fifth, Parker went on to reach his 34th hundred (and his first at Hastings), and had reached 117 before he was finally caught at slip by Tavare. Sussex batted on until just before the tea interval for a total of 322 – only 2 runs short of their highest score for the season, thus setting Kent a modest 106 to win off the 35 overs available. This seemed a formality for a side on a winning streak at the top of the table, but Sussex were to fight all the way. Wickets fell steadily at 14-1, 29-2, 43-3, 72-4, 87-5, and 102-6, and when the last over came up 4 runs were still required. Penn flicked the first ball to the fine leg boundary, and Kent had just made it. Parker had courageously used Clarke – the only leg-break bowler in county cricket – over the last stages. It was a wonderful fight back by Sussex after that disastrous first innings of 71.

In recent years there have been some fine encounters at Hastings, and may the final one v Middlesex this year be just as thrilling – the last match ever to be played on this historic turf before stumps are drawn for ever.

Sunday League Cricket

The creation of this '40 over' League in 1969 offered the people of East Sussex a chance to see this hectic but popular form of county cricket. From 1969 to 1986 it was known as the 'John Player League', and since 1987 as the 'Refuge Assurance League'. Here is a record of the matches played at Hastings, with a mention of good Sussex performances.

1969	—		
1970	—		
1971	—		
1972	—		
1973	v Yorkshire	lost	
1974	v Worcester	won	J J Groome 64, A Buss 'hat trick'
1975	v Warwickshire	lost	A W Greig 108*
1976	—		
1977	v Derbyshire	won	M A Buss 78, R D V Knight 76*
1978	v Glamorgan	lost	Imran Khan 54
1979	v Lancashire	won	Miandad 98*, H Phillipson 71
1980	v Essex	won	P Parker 73, C M Wells 65*
1981	v Northants	lost	
1982	v Glamorgan	won	G Le Roux 88 (in 42 m), C M Wells 81

1983	v Northants	won	P Parker 121*
1984	v Kent	lost	
1985	v Lancashire	won	Imran Khan 80*, A M Green 70
1986	v Northants	lost	
1987	v Lancashire	(no play)	
1988	v Hampshire	(no play)	

4 · Festival Cricket

Festival cricket originates from a match a Scarborough in 1871 between C I Thornton's team of visitors and an eleven raised by Lord Londesborough. This soon became a regular fixture on the ground which is still privately owned by Scarborough Cricket Club. The selectors picked teams which gave a chance to county players to have some end-of-season holiday cricket; they could indulge in carefree stroke-play to the entertainment of themselves and of the many spectators who welcomed the local practice of the club of covering the wicket to avoid delay after rain and of abandoning the tea interval to save time.

So began the famous Scarborough Festival, earlier known as the 'Carnival'. It grew rapidly in popularity and drew spectators from far and wide, many of whom made this an annual holiday pilgrimage. To be invited as a player to all the fun at Scarborough was an honour almost akin to Test selection, and proved that you had the proper attitude to the game both on and off the field. C I Thornton, H D G Leveson-Gower, and later T N Pearce were the supremos.

The Scarborough Festival continues to flourish after over a hundred years, though now some of the time is given up to yet more one-day revelry. It was a sad blow to festival cricket when a few years ago visiting touring teams – the main attraction of the week – decided to return home immediately after the last Test match. One reason was to get some holiday break before setting off on the next stage of the touring merry-go-round; the other was that some teams objected to having to face at Scarborough what was virtually another Test eleven when all the hard play was meant to be over.

Festival cricket is a difficult game. The match must be very keen, yet entertaining, but never become farcical. The first time a bun was bowled instead of a ball it might have been funny, but this could not be repeated. Players with some flair for being amusing could play to the gallery, but not too often. Victory must be sought, but not too soon – ideally in the last moments of the third day, and yet play must not seem to be too obviously spun out. It was pleasant if certain players could reach seasonal targets such as 100 wickets or 2000 runs, but they must not be given undue favour.

W G Grace once invited criticism when in a festival match at Hastings in 1900 he kept C L Townsend on to bowl over after over. Before he game Townsend had 95 wickets and needed 5 more to add 100 wickets to his 2,000 runs. He at last finished up with an analysis of 54.5-8-163-5, so he reached his target; the other bowlers together bowled 70 overs in an innings of 331.

When writing about his first appearances in festival cricket at Scarborough G L Jessop said that he expected to find a lot of gratuitous full-pitches and half-volleys served up, but he did not find any such courtesy. Only once did he find any serious lapse from the proprieties of real cricket. This was in the match between the Home Counties and the Rest of England at Hastings in 1899 when on the last afternoon – a Saturday with a full crowd – and little hope of a finish, he had reached 30* just before the tea interval and dashed out to a lob from Jephson, missed the ball and made what he knew was a quite hopeless dash back. He was surprised to hear the voice of old Bob Thoms, the umpire, say: 'Not out, not out!' As he carefully reaffixed the bails he muttered: 'Sixpenny crowd – Saturday gate – can't disappoint 'em – near thing – near thing – but not near enough for the occasion!' Jessop ended up with a score of 100* and the huge crowd went home happy.

The success of the game at Hastings between the Australians and the South of England in 1886 suggested that there might be scope for a Hastings Festival on the lines of the one at Scarborough. Mr Carless and Captain Greatrex worked hard to plan for a festival in 1887 in which there was one three-day game between the North and South followed by two two-day games between the Gentlemen of Sussex and the Gentlemen of Surrey, and the Gentlemen of Sussex v the Players of Sussex.

The North v South game started 'under favourable auspicies'. The townspeople had been invited to decorate their houses with bunting and there were extensive decorations in Breeds Place, High Street, and Queens Road. The railway company assisted the promoters by issuing cheap tickets from most places between London and Hastings. In those days cricket weeks really were something special. Apart from the actual play there was an embarassing choice of other activities. For example: displays of Grecian Dancing; amateur theatricals; a Ball (dance with the cricketers!); several bands (including a Red Hungarian one); a male voice choir; floral baskets in abundance; illuminations by 3,000 patent prismatic lamps; oriental lanterns hung in festoons. But Hastings never quite matched an item seen once at Tunbridge Wells when there was a firework display with a set-piece showing Frank Woolley, batting – unfortunately – right-handed.

The whole week was a grand occasion full of colours matched only by the splendour of the caps of the numerous amateurs. Even the horse dragging the roller wore bright badges, and the bands round the many straw hats of the spectators glittered when joyfully thrown up in the air at the sight of some rousing stroke. It was all one big festivity.

Most important was the weather. Before the game of North v South in 1887 it had been unsettled, but now the opening day 'was beautifully fine with a rising barometer and a favourable wind'. About 2,000 people flocked into the ground, producing as much as £100 in receipts. To accommodate them: 'A commodious stand with covered roof capable of seating 500 people was erected on the Queens Road side of the ground. The wicket prepared by A T Manwaring, the ground man, was worthy of the high praise showered upon it by competent authorities'.

The teams were strong and included three local players, H Pigg, A M Sutthery, and Harry Phillips. Mr W W Read won the toss against Tom Emmett, the North's captain, and batted when play began at 12.30. The South batted steadily to be all out for 210, but the North were bowled out for only 119, and 'of course' had to follow on. The 'of course' is a reminder that in those days a deficit of 80 runs on the first innings meant a compulsory follow-on. The Law gave no choice. The North now batted better with a score of 203, leaving the South only 113 to win, but now because of the follow-on, they had to bat last, and the excellent bowling of Peate and Emmett was too good for them. They were all out for 85 and lost by 27 runs. Though the other games were not so well attended, the Festival was successfully launched and continued to function (except in 1906) until the final matches of 1969 – a fair spell. This was thanks to all the many local organisers, and especially to the enthusiasm of William Carless who continued to act as secretary until his retirement in 1908. Over this stretch of time the Australians appeared nine times, and the South Africans once. The other games were made up of scratch teams, such as North v South, Gentlemen v Players, or such hybrids as 'Kent and Sussex', The Home Counties, or somebody's XI. The strength of the sides varied, and sometimes it was linked to the demands of Scarborough, where the selectors tended to have first choice. Carless had always stated that the success of any festival depended on the quality of the players. One player whose support was essential was W G Grace. The position and importance of W G must be made quite clear, so here is a full account of this colossus.

W G Grace

It is difficult today to realise just how much W G Grace did to develop the game of cricket into a nationwide spectacle. When he first came into big cricket in 1865 at the age of 16 there was little county cricket, and the game was supported by comparatively few. Within a decade his reputation led people to come to look upon him as a phenomenon. Not until Bradman was there any other cricketer able to exert such a universal attraction. WG really made the modern game.

The early days of WG's cricket were often played on very rough pitches against a host of fast bowlers exploiting the conditions to the full, and up to the 1870s all hits had to be run out, with few boundaries. In spite of these difficulties WG in first-class cricket between 1865 and 1876 scored nearly 17,000 runs at the amazing average of 55.59. No other batsman of this period reached an average even of 25, or had surpassed his contemporaries so emphatically until, again – Bradman.

W G Grace in his late twenties. Author's Collection

W G Grace went on playing in first-class cricket until his last match in 1908 when he was nearly 60. He simply loved to play cricket and when, after leaving Gloucestershire, it seemed that his playing days were at last over, he formed his own club called 'London County'. Because of the length of his career and the many photos taken of him in his later years, we tend to think of Grace as an overweight lumbering old man, and forget that he had once been a superb athlete. In spite of his thickening waistline WG remained to the last an outstanding draw; with his famous black beard and his gaudy MCC cap he was the most easily recognised man in all England. It is a true story that on some grounds the admission fee was increased 'if Dr Grace plays', but many would have been ready to pay almost anything to see the great man in action.

It is clear that if a new festival were to succeed then the support of WG was vital, and though he did not play in the inaugural week of 1887, he appeared in the next year and continued to play until his last appearance in 1905. Hastings had however seen the Doctor play long before 1888. We have read how way back in 1875 he scored 210 against an XVIII of Hastings, and in doing so made a famous hit out of the ground. He once made another such hit off the bowling of Briggs in a North v South match at Hastings in 1895. C W Wright, an old friend who was the good-natured butt of many cricketers, decided to play a joke on WG. After this hit, he bribed a small boy to run out from the boundary right on to the pitch, as if sent by the scorers to enquire the name of the batsman (as often seen in a minor match). WG gave the information in stentorian tones, and guessing the identity of the instigator, added: 'You can tell Chawles that he is more of a fool than I took him to be.' There was always plenty of schoolboy banter when WG was about.

In 1877 when cricket seemed to be at a low ebb at Hastings, Henry Cousins, editor of the local *Observer*, decided on his own to approach WG and to ask him to consider bringing another United South of England XI down to Hastings. Cousins had previously called a meeting and found some supporters ready to guarantee a guinea each to promote the match. Having fixed a fee to be paid in advance the ever-shrewd WG agreed to come, and collected a strong team which included his ill-fated younger brother G F Grace, as well as Midwinter from Australia, R Humphrey, Jupp and Pooley from Surrey, his cousin W R Gilbert and James Lillywhite and Charlwood from Sussex.

The enterprise of Henry Cousins (later to become the author of *Hastings of Bygone Days and the Present* – 1911) was well rewarded: 'There has seldom been seen such a crowd at the Central Ground as was witnessed during the three days of the match'.

But disaster had threatened in the form of a hurricane that swept the ground during the lunch interval on the second day. WG however, who was not out before the storm, continued to bat on when play was resumed. He had asked Henry Cousins, the promoter, if he had any special request. Cousins' reply was that all he wanted was a long innings for the entertainment of the crowd. WG obliged, the spectators had a fine treat, and interest in cricket at Hastings revived so well that an Australian team was invited to come in the following year.

W Carless, who originated the festival in 1887, had admitted that getting the co-operation of WG was essential for success. Carless got this, and WG appeared year after year, usually as captain. He was now aged 40 and was reaching the stage when he was being known as 'the old man' rather than as 'WG', but his very presence was magnetic as ever, he could still trundle up those deceptive round-arm balls, and he remained the canniest of captains.

From his first festival game in 1888 until his last appearance in 1905 WG played in 31 matches. He made two centuries – a really fine innings of 131 out of the Gentlemen's total of 247 in 1893, and a score of 104 in the next year when he and Stoddart put on 150 for the first wicket. In subsequent games he became less successful, but it should be remembered that he was now in his fifties. Over the whole spell of his festival matches he missed only one match, in 1896 when he was too lame. In the later days he tended to get out after scoring fifty: in his 52 innings he was caught 23 times, bowled 22 times (Richardson getting him 7 times, 5 of them bowled): he was LBW only twice, once stumped, and never run out.

Rhodes has a story to tell of one of the LBW dismissals. In the North v South match of 1900 WG had scored 5 when Rhodes made a confident appeal for LBW. He says: 'The Doctor just stood his ground, and looked as if nothing had happened, but Bob Thoms, the umpire saw that there would be no misunderstanding. 'You're out, you're out, you're out', he cried three times. 'You'll have to go', so of course WG went, though he did not look as if he liked it'.

WG practices in front of the pavilion at Hastings. Author's Collection

In spite of occasional differences of opinion WG always regarded Bob Thoms as 'The Prince of Umpires'.

No doubt in Festival games LBW decisions are less frequent than in county matches, and some umpires were reluctant to give WG out. He once retorted to an umpire: 'People have come to see me bat, not to see you umpire'. Bob Thoms was certainly not one to be scared of WG. He and H Carpenter were the two best-known umpires of the day, stood in almost every match of the whole series of Festival games, and played a significant role in their success. The staunch work of umpires is too often taken for granted. In later Festivals Frank Chester's part was just as important: he enjoyed coming to Hastings, and said that he preferred it to Scarborough.

WG's dominant influence was ever present, and in one match it is alleged that Schofield Haigh of Yorkshire asked permission of WG to depart from the game early. Not long before the moment arrived when he hoped he could leave he was fielding at short-leg and WG was batting. He skied a soft catch towards Haigh and shouted out: 'If you catch it, I shan't let you go home early.' Haigh deliberately missed the catch, but he did not miss his train.

A common scene of WG at Hastings was the horde of small boys who followed the great man whenever he came out of the Pavilion to go for a practice knock. When the craze for autographs became fashionable that of WG was naturally in great demand, and he was always ready to oblige the young who are the most persistent of all hero-worshippers. One boy obtained his autograph at Hastings and then at Lord's some weeks later the same boy approached WG for his autograph. He recognised the boy's book and pen, and taxed the boy with already having obtained his autograph. The boy pleaded guilty, but explained: 'Yes, Sir, but I swapped that for a Bishop and Dan Leno.'

G L Jessop

If W G Grace was the figure-head of festival cricket at Hastings there is no doubt that the star was Gilbert Jessop. Before describing some of his festival efforts, consider for a moment his overall achievement:

– He scored his runs at the rate of just under 80 runs an hour. Over the years the average rate for a batsman is about 27, and the next highest among great batsmen is 55 an hour by Trumper and Woolley. Many of Botham's innings match Jessop for speed and sixes.

– In his 179 innings of 50 or over, only once did he bat for over three hours (a matter of 240 scored in 200 minutes), only 10 times did he bat for more than two hours, and only 35 times for more than an hour and a half. His average time for reaching a hundred was 72 minutes.

– He was also a fine fast bowler and one of the all-time greats as a fielder at cover point.

Gilbert Jessop was a perky bright-eyed man of 5ft 7in with india-rubber double-jointed limbs and wrists of steel, and was filled with an indomitable spirit of attack.

No wonder he was the ideal choice for any cricket festival, but before he first honoured Hastings in 1898 he had played for several years at the Scarborough Festival with very little success: in fact in his first 12 innings there he collected only 69 runs with an average of 5.75 and a top score of 13. Hastings brought him a wonderful change of form, and in 33 innings played there he scored 1,592 runs at an average of 56.85, including 6 centuries, the most ever scored at Hastings by any batsman.

This remarkable average was the result of very consistent batting. Festival cricket by its very nature discourages high individual scoring, but Jessop hardly ever failed. After making centuries in the weeks of 1898, 1899, 1900 and 1902 he excelled all these in an innings of 159* v the South Africans in 1904. Though not yet granted Test match status, they were a very strong side. Jessop did not really want to play in this match because

Gilbert Jessop ready for action. Author's Collection

of an attack of lumbago, but he obliged and went in 5th after 3 wickets had fallen for 18 runs; wickets continued to fall, and when the 7th wicket fell at 80, Jessop had scored 36* in 43 minutes. Shortly before he had asked the South African captain if he might have a runner. The captain was Frank Mitchell, under whose captaincy Jessop had played for Cambridge in 1896.

Let him tell the story: 'GLJ came in saying, "Oh, Mike (my nickname), my rheumatism is awful. May I have a runner?" "Right," said I. In about 10 minutes he was running halfway up the wickets to J J Kotze, who bowled as fast as Larwood. He got 150 odd. I was had properly, but they did not often catch me like that.'

Before long George Cox came in and defending stoutly helped Jessop to add 104 runs in the last 45 minutes before lunch. Jessop had reached 50* in 57 minutes and then added 50 more in 15 minutes while Cox scored 1. At lunch the score was 184-7 of which Jessop had made 130*. After lunch his lumbago had worn off, his runner dismissed, and he continued to go down the wicket to Kotze, who in Plum Warner's opinion was second in sheer pace only to the legendary Kortright. The faster Kotze bowled, the harder Jessop hit him, and fielders were strung out everywhere. So audacious was Jessop in advancing that the wicket-keeper began to stand up to Kotze on the off chance of a stumping. He had never done this before. The tail enders tried to stay in with Jessop but the innings was over at 237, Jessop being left with a score of 159* made put of 219 in just over 2 hours. He had hit 26 fours, and no one will ever know how many of these cleared the ropes.

If this hundred was a remarkable one, there was an ever greater one to follow. On 29 August 1907, Gloucestershire played a county match as part of the festival and Jessop scored 119. A few days later there was a match between the Gentlemen of the South against the Players of the South. The Gents batted first and made 211 to which Jessop provided a rare duck, clean bowled second ball by an off-break from Fairservice, who felt he had done the wrong thing, such was the obvious disappointment of the crowd. In their second innings the Gentlemen's 3rd wicket went down at 25 just before lunch. When play was resumed Jessop came in at 2.15 facing a 'pair', and it was Fairservice bowling again. The first ball however was a full pitch and was driven to the boundary, likewise the next ball. To quote Fairservice: 'Jessop thereupon let down his hair and gave a display which dismayed us all'.

Seeing that Jessop looked like business, Albert Relf, one of the steadiest bowlers in England, suggested to his captain that he could 'get rid of the bloke'. Jessop possibly heard this remark: Relf's first ball ended up on a roof in Station Road, and the next five went for four each. The over produced 26 runs and Relf retired amid great hilarity. Within 35 minutes of the resumption of play after lunch the total had risen by 108 runs, 87 of them to Jessop. He reached his hundred just before 3 o'clock after batting for 42 minutes (only two minutes slower than a hundred he had once made against Yorkshire). To quote a report: 'Changes in the bowling now seemed desirable, but it was all the same to Jessop, and a gigantic pull into the garden of one of the houses in Devonshire Road brought his score to 154*, scored in 63 minutes – the fastest score of 150 ever made. Soon after he made his only miss-hit which sent the ball up near square-leg; Frank Woolley made a valiant run for it, but failed to hold the ball. This seemed to slow Jessop down as he took 27 more minutes to take his score to 191, and he then skied a ball from Woolley to deep mid-off where Butt made a most dodgy catch by holding the ball between his knees after much frantic juggling. This unlucky dismissal prevented Jessop from reaching a double century in a new record time – the record then being held by himself when he scored the first 200 runs of his 286 v Sussex in 1903 in just two hours.

Jessop had scored his 191 out of 234 in 90 minutes between 2.15 and 3.45. He had hit 5 sixes – all out of the ground, 30 fours, 2 threes, 10 twos, and only 15 singles. In a letter written much later, Jessop recalled this innings: 'I remember at Hastings in 1907 hitting 5 balls out of the ground as well as 11 others over the ropes which would have increased my score from 191 to 213. I would have enriched my bag of centuries by more than one if the easier reward had been in vogue at that time. (ie 6 runs given for hits over the ropes). I apologise for talking about my past deeds, a fault I rarely indulge in'. It was never easy to get Jessop to talk about himself.

There was not much coverage by the Press of this innings, but some of the London papers produced such headlines as 'Terrific hitting by Jessop – scores 191 in 90 minutes', 'Hurricane hitting by "the Wonder" at Hastings – Rough on Relf', and *The Globe* burst out into a poem which included the lines:

> We do not yawn, Believe me, that's
> But seldom done when Jessop bats!

When Jessop was on the attack, even a single yawn could miss something. Nothing he ever did surpassed those magical 90 minutes on 3 September 1907. Among the spectators was the cricket writer, G D Martineau, then a small boy. He once wrote: 'Jessop hit the ball it seems to me now out of every side of the ground, not merely over the boundary, but into the street among trams and horses – a wonderful thing. I came back that evening with my mind in a doze of wonder, and subsequently ruined much of my cricket by imitating Jessop's crouch and seeking to cart balls for six in his highly unorthodox manner'. Lucky Martineau and indeed all those spectators who witnessed all the many festival games at Hastings in which Jessop was seen at his best.

Cartoon of Jessop after his great 191 in 1907.

Let the local paper have the last word on Jessop's 191: 'An otherwise insignificant match was redeemed by some bright play by Jessop.'

Between 1887 and 1909 there were 42 games organised by the Festival committee, and these produced a magnificent array of great players. Here are the stories of a handful of these matches selected as specially interesting because of close finishes, dramatic turns of fortune, or memorable performances.

Gentlemen v Players   16, 17, 18 September 1889

The first really tight finish came in the match between the Gentlemen and Players, whose side included such notable performers as W Gunn, R Abel, W Barnes, A Ward, R Peel, G Ulyett, W Attewell, G A Lohmann, and M Sherwin – all England cricketers: however, few of them did well, and in the last innings the Gentlemen needed only 73 runs to win. The pitch was now badly worn, and the Gentlemen suffered a severe setback when Grace was out 'c Gunn, b Lohmann 6'; a fine hit looked like clearing the boundary, but Gunn reached the ball just in time, and amid loud cheers plucked it out of the air with his left hand. At lunch the score was a hopeless 25-5, and Attewell and Lohmann were turning the ball sharply. W W Read and E J McCormick tried to stem the tide, but when the ninth wicket fell 8 runs were still needed.

The young local amateur kept his head, and when Lohmann bowled his first loose ball, a long-hop to leg, McCormick hit it for four, and he followed this by sending a ball from Attewell to square-leg for another boundary. So amid a scene of wild excitement and hats flying in the air, the Gentlemen won by 1 wicket, McCormick ending up with 25*. He was publicly presented with a new bat by the Mayor who congratulated a local fellow on carrying off the honours.

The financial records of the earlier games of the Festival are revealing:

Year	Receipts	Expend	Gain	Australian share of Loss	Gate
	£	£	£	£	£
1887	395	407	—	12	—
1888	680	650	30	—	203
1889	704	676	28	—	—
1890	868	708	160	—	214
1891	763	619	144	—	—
1892	728	643	85	—	—
1893	904	812	92	—	182
1894	763	746	17	—	—
1895	1,156	853	303	—	—
1896	901	983	—	82	230
1897	687	775	—	88	—
1898	821	789	32	—	—
1899	969	1,031	—	62	300
1900	898	877	21	—	—
1901	790	836	—	46	—
1902	1,045	1,061	—	15	280

The Australians seemed to have done very well out of it. The sums of money seem to us now to be trivial, but the profits were satisfactory enough to encourage the committee to continue. So much depended on the weather; every hold-up through rain threatened to wreck the budget, and a blank day was a calamity.

Gentlemen v Players   12, 13, 14 September 1892

In delightful weather two very strong teams had been got together for a match that fluctuated dramatically. The Gentlemen were dismissed for 211, chiefly by Attewell and Lohmann. This was a poor score for a side with a batting order that began: W G Grace, H T Hewitt, A E Stoddart, L C H Palairet, W W Read, and Sir Timothy O'Brien. The only inexperienced member was the local player G K Papillon, of Crowhurst Park, who came in for the injured J J Ferris.

Part of poster of the festival of 1890. Hastings Museum & Art Gallery

The Players were all out for 109, thanks to a tremendous effort by S M J Woods who bowled through the innings for an analysis of 26.1-10-46-8. Following-on the Players fought back to reach a score of 388-7, and then at last Ulyett declared. Sammy Woods again did most of the bowling, and ended up with the extraordinary figures of 65-15-201-3: the other supporting bowlers had 71 overs with little success. So Woods bowled – and at a fast pace – almost unchanged, 'keeping on in the pluckiest fashion and having distressing luck'. The Gentlemen were now set 287 to win in only 155 minutes; the declaration came too late to make a game of it. They ended up at 131-7.

The Australians v The South of England
7, 8, 9 September 1893

On the previous day the Australians had been in the field at Scarborough, had enjoyed little sleep on the long journey to Hastings, and when they had to bat first, they were all out for 64; Lockwood 6-43 and Richardson 4-20 bowled unchanged. The South with 8 England players did rather better with 147 (Hewitt 58), and in their second innings, the Australians thanks to a dashing 75 by J J Lyons, managed to reach 193. Richardson now took 7 wickets for 83 – 5 of them clean bowled – and I am sure he would have put Hastings high on his list of favourite grounds.

South of England v The Australians 1893
(back row) R Carpenter (umpire), Mr A E Stoddart, T Richardson, J T Hearne,
Mr Carless (Hon Sec), R A Thoms (umpire)
(sitting) Mr W W Read, W H Lockwood, Dr W G Grace, Mr H T Hewett, Mr J J Ferris, Rev A P Wickham
(on ground) A Hearne, Rev H C L Tindall

The South of England v the Australians 1893. Trustees of the Central Ground

This left the South 111 to win; Ferris was out for 0, but Hewitt, a lusty left-hander, made 36 and Stoddart 27, and in spite of the bowling of Turner, Trumble and Giffen, the South won a most creditable victory by 4 wickets. What a memory for a local player in the South team: he was the Rev H C L Tindall, later Headmaster of Hurst Court School on The Ridge, St Leonards.

The North v The South   11, 12, 13 September 1893

The second game of the week provided some truly spectacular play. At the end of the first two innings the South seemed to be heading for victory: with a score of 251 they had a lead of 93, and then promptly took three North wickets for only 8 runs (Richardson and Lockwood again on the war-path). When the 5th wicket fell at 79, the North were still 14 runs behind. At this point C E de Trafford and E Smith came together. In only an hour and three-quarters later, the score had risen to 333. de Trafford was then stumped just on the close of play for 110. He had put on 254 runs for the 6th wicket with Smith. de Trafford was brother-in-law of the great

84

batsman Sir T C O'Brien, and a dashing hitter who captained Leicester from 1890 to 1906. This was his highest innings to date.

The hitting of Ernest Smith was even more vigorous. He made no mistake until he had reached 94. He was 144* overnight, but next day he was soon out 'c Stoddart, b Richardson' for 154. He had scored his runs in only 2 hours and 5 minutes, chiefly with a six (out of the ground), a 5 and 21 fours (many of which landed over the boundary). Ernest Smith played in over 150 games for Yorkshire in limited appearances because he was a schoolmaster. He was a powerful hitter and a fast bowler, who played his last first-class match at Eastbourne in 1928, at the advanced age of 58. This extraordinary stand with de Trafford was said by *Wisden* to be a feat of fast-scoring 'without parallel in a match of importance'. It still remains one of the fastest stands on record.

The South were now faced with the unexpectedly large task of scoring 261, and in the end they lost the game by 25 runs – an amazing match. Ernest Smith added 3 more wickets to the 5 he had taken in the first innings. He will not have forgotten this match.

The Rest of England v A E Stoddart's England XI to Australia 1898
(back row) R Carpenter (umpire), Mr C J Kortright, Mr A E Stoddart, Mr C L Townsend,
Mr G L Jessop, H R Butt, R A Thoms (umpire)
(sitting) W Brockwell, A Shrewsbury, Dr W G Grace, Mr F G J Ford, Mr G Brann
(on ground) R Abel, W Rhodes

The Rest v A E Stoddart's England XI 1898. Trustees of the Central Ground

A E Stoddart's England XI v The Rest 5, 6, 7 September 1898

In 1895 Stoddart had brought to Hastings the side he had led in Australia, and he now again reassembled the team he had taken there in the previous winter. The Rest had a batting order that read: Abel, Brockwell, F G J Ford, Shrewsbury, W G Grace, C L Townsend, G Brann, G L Jessop, C J Kortright, Rhodes and Butt; almost every player in the game had an England cap. It was possibly the finest collection of players ever seen at Hastings. Batting first, The Rest opened badly against Richardson, but Grace made 58 and the total reached 236. Stoddard's side did little better with 261, being kept in control by Rhodes and Kortright, who made a contrasting pair of opening bowlers such as is seldom seen today – very fast right and slow left. On going in again, The Rest lost 4 wickets for 17, all ducks by Abel, Brockwell, Grace and Townsend. Then came a typical Jessop innings of 112* in 70 minutes off the bowling of Richardson, J T Hearne, Briggs and Hirst – a formidable quartet. But the total was only 206, and Stoddart's side were able to knock off the runs for the loss of 5 wickets.

Surrey & Sussex v The Rest of England
8, 9, 10 September 1898

The second game of the week was finely balanced, and memorable for the batting of D L A Jephson in the Surrey/Sussex first innings. In a total of 254 he scored 143 in 110 minutes, the last 33 coming in only 10 minutes: 'it was quite worthy of comparison with a Jessop display', wrote *Wisden*. After giving two chances before he had reached 40, he made not the slightest mistake. He hit 29 fours and his score reads:

> 424441 4114144 3414 4414444221 241444414422 444141 414

The Rest replied with 176; after a fine start by Grace 40 and MacLaren 72, they collapsed with Richardson again excelling with 8-62. The Surrey/Sussex side then squandered their lead of 78 by being dismissed for 141, mainly by J T Hearne, who with figures of 6-72 'bowled as though his summer's work was just beginning'. The Rest began the task of scoring 220 in some trouble, but thanks to Townsend 51 and Hirst 35* they got home with 4 wickets to spare. So ended a most successful week.

The North v The South 6, 7, 8 September 1900

Though Fry and Ranji were absent, the North and South had such strong batting sides that the game ended in a draw after a run-getting spree of 1,227 runs scored at the rate of 96 runs an hour. On the third day 473 runs came in just over 4½ hours. J T Tyldesley had 121 on the opening day, and later made a second hundred before lunch: this was the first time at Hastings a player had scored two hundreds in a match. The South, whose

86

reply to the North's innings of 440 was far behind with 287, would have been much worse off but for D L A Jephson's century (124), which followed his taking 5 wickets with his lobs. His 51 in the second innings would surely have made him 'man of the match' if such 'heroes' had existed then. Another candidate would have been Jessop whose 4-87 enabled him to reach his 100 wickets for the season. He had already made 2,000 runs and he added to these with a second innings score of 123*. The last day became rather unreal when Lord Hawke gave Rhodes only 9 overs, and at one time allowed the South to score 141 runs without changing the bowling. The game provided the crowd with a feast of batting, but too many runs to bring a result.

Gentlemen v Players   9, 10, 11 September 1901

To quote *Wisden*: 'the second match of the week was truly sensational in character, the Players being robbed by rain of almost certain victory after being 168 runs behind on the first innings'. On the opening day the Gentlemen made a formidable 406 with a century from A O Jones, 54 from WG and 45 in 20 minutes from Jessop. The next day the Players replied with 238 of which J T Tyldesley scored 96 thus just missing three consecutive hundreds at Hastings. The bowlers, J H Sinclair, the South African, and J R Mason, bowled 31 overs unchanged through an innings of 238, a strange spell of endurance at any time let alone a Festival game. With a lead of 168 and the follow-on no longer compulsory, WG decided to bat again, force the pace and set the Players a large target. I suppose too that he did not want to risk the game finishing early. The plan misfired utterly, for against the bowling of Hirst 3-38 and Rhodes 6-27, the Gentlemen were all out in 80 minutes for a paltry 59. There were fine catches, some over-audacious batting, and Rhodes made the most of it. The Players needed 228 runs to win, but owing to interruption by rain ended up 51 short.

Kent & Sussex v The Rest   4, 5, 6 September 1902

Though (as often) some leading players were engaged at Scarborough two good teams were selected for what turned out to be a very close game. On the opening day the hybrid team with an odd-looking batting order were out for 184, chiefly to the opening bowlers, Gill (fast) and Braund (leg-breaks). The Rest began shockingly, the first four batsmen, Grace, C J B Wood, Braund and McGahey being out for scores of 9, 9, 0, and 0. Then came Jessop and his chanceless 109 made in 80 minutes enabled the total to reach 231. The Kent & Sussex side started badly with Fry failing again, but by the close they were 79 runs on with 2 wickets down: next day however only 98 more runs were added, and The Rest were left with 178 to win. Wood and Braund were out for 0 in Tate's first over, but Grace played one of his best innings at Hastings, and when out for 70 at 145-7, victory was in sight. This Trott and J Gunn together swiftly achieved.

In 1907 the Festival Week included one county match against Gloucestershire, and indeed Hastings was honoured with three first-class matches since Somerset had come in July, and there was another game to follow.

The Festival authorities excelled themselves with the general entertainment. There was the usual band near the Station Road top entrance playing such engaging items as: The Glow-worm, The Nigger's Birthday, Dear Erin, and Miss Hook of Holland; flags of both counties flew at the masthead. Then there were the tents; for the first time the Freemasons had taken a tent 'which looked very pretty both externally and internally'. All the tents were 'procured from a well-known London firm and looked spick and span', but the clear winner was that of the local MP, Harvey du Cros. It was like a vast flower-show, with the plants listed in full with Latin names, and the centre-piece consisted of a superb basket of white spider lilies (*Pancratium fragrans*).

It was considered that 'a more beautiful private tent had never been seen at any festival, and the guests were treated right royally'. It would perhaps be ungallant to liken it to some present-day sponsors' tents with the booze and piped-music flowing freely among the plastic palms, but no doubt many of the MP's visitors were more interested in the social side than in the actual play. There was good cricket also, with a Jessop century, to be followed shortly by his historic innings of 191 which has already been described.

The MCC Australian XI v An England XI
3, 4, 5 September 1908

This was the third time that an MCC Australian touring team had appeared in the Festival, and it was very sad that rain prevented any play on the last day. The England XI were all out for 161 on the first day, Blythe and Rhodes bowling 32 overs each unchanged. When did two slow left-handers last do such a thing? Only an innings of 64 by Ranji (now H H Jam Sahib of Nawanagar) saved them from disaster. The MCC team then collapsed for 107 to the bowling of Jessop 3-43 and Arnold 7-51. After that the weather took a hand with frequent interruptions. The England XI made 87-7 and declared, with Rhodes and Blythe once again bowling unchanged. In the short time remaining MCC scored 41-4 and that was that. In spite of the weather the spectators had the chance of seeing most of the greatest players in the land, since apart from the MCC side, the England XI consisted of Fry, Warner, Jessop, S H Day, the Rev F H Gillingham, Ranji, J R Mason, Lilley, Arnold, A E Relf, and Field. Would that England had a reserve team of such quality today.

88

The Festival Week of 1909 was the last until the post-war revival of 1946. It seems that it was increasingly hard to get together really good sides, and according to an article in *The Cricketer* in 1921, the Hastings Festival came to an end owing to 'unpunctuality and irresponsibility'. It may have just run out of steam. The loss of the Festival was however soon compensated by the Sussex County authorities being persuaded to play regular county matches at Hastings.

Though the Festival was not to revive until after the Second World War, there were occasional non-county first-class games after 1909. In 1912 both the Australian and South African teams played against scratch sides at Hastings, and in 1919 the Australian Imperial Forces team played against a South of England XI and lost. Next year the ground authorities contrived to arrange a match between the North and South. This game was chiefly notable for a stand of 141 in 80 minutes between Hobbs 66 and Woolley 90. No great player has got out in the nineties more often than Woolley; he never troubled to approach a hundred with special care, but just went on freely playing his strokes. In 1921 the all-powerful Australians visited Hastings and scored massively (Armstrong 182*). Then the quartet of Gregory, McDonald, Mailey and Armstrong shot out the South of England for two low scores, though Maurice Tate in only his second representative game had the pleasure of hitting Armstrong twice for six – a foretaste of what enjoyment he was later to bring to spectators at Hastings.

In 1922 the RAF Club planned to arrange a cricket festival to help raise funds, and the chief organiser was P G H Fender, the Surrey captain. After a week at Eastbourne, it was decided to switch the Festival to Hastings next year. The first game, 'Capped v Uncapped', would have made a valuable Test Trial if it had been played a few months earlier, but the last week of September was getting too late both for the public and the weather. Maurice Tate took 11 wickets and another 'uncapped' hero was Herbert Sutcliffe who made a century.

In the following season of 1924 the RAF Festival gained status by having the touring South Africans play the South of England, and in the second match Lord Cowdray's XI met the Rest of England. In this game there was a spectacular knock by Robert Relf who scored 114 out of 147 in 75 minutes with 7 sixes and 11 fours; in the same innings G W Stephens, a Warwickshire amateur, made 121 in 85 minutes. Later Arthur Gilligan had his first long spell of bowling since his serious accident in July. Perhaps unwisely he bowled unchanged through Lord Cowdray's second innings for an analysis of 36-10-90-7.

Though the festival was a success, an earlier date meant a clash with the Scarborough officials over invitations. Some players said they preferred Hastings to Scarborough, but sadly it was decided to let the RAF Festival come to an end.

The RAF week may have suggested the regular return of festival cricket to Hastings, but competition elsewhere was making team selection increasingly difficult; with varying degrees of success, Blackpool, Bournemouth and Folkestone all made attempts at a festival week. So that was the end of the Hastings Festival until the post-war revival in 1946, and from then until 1966 there was an annual week. In every year (except 1965) the overseas touring teams appeared – always an attraction – and the other match tended to become a contest between a star-studded Commonwealth XI against a scratch side such as (most frequently) A E R Gilligan's XI, or L E G Ames's XI.

The revival of the Festival in 1946 was the brain-child of Wing-Commander A J Holmes, one time captain of Sussex and manager of the MCC's last pre-war tour to South Africa in 1938-9. He formed a Committee including A E R Gilligan, Sir Pelham Warner, and C B Fry, with George Lay its excellent secretary. Spectators starved of big cricket since 1939 relished the idea of seeing the great players enjoying themselves and felt that they too were playing some special part in the fun. There was a general air of bonhomie – no partisan anxiety of a county match – just sit back and relish a leisurely day's cricket – all passion spent. Such was the feeling:

Get your deck chair at the right notch (that all right for you behind?). It was all so friendly and relaxed. Make sure the sandwiches and flask are safely at hand, and the score-card tucked away. Light up the pipe – look, Mabel, here come the umpires – the sun shines and heaven is at hand. When some usually dour opening batsman opens his shoulders a comment might be made to a stranger sitting alongside – reminiscences begin (and what does it really matter if he will talk about 'Jack' Langridge when he means 'John'). Lunchtime comes and the refreshments vanish all too swiftly, but this means time for the traditional stroll to inspect the pitch and make a few enlightened comments, but 'Oh, there's old Tom – not seen you for ages'. Festival cricket really could be an occasion of great joy, especially in those early post-war seasons.

India v South of England   4, 5, 6 September 1946

The attractive Indian team was given a warm welcome when they came to meet a strong South of England side that included Leslie Ames, George Cox, J D Robertson, B H Valentine, H T Bartlett, S C Griffith, R T D Perks and Tom Goddard. In an exciting match the Indians with scores of 241 (Merchant 82) and 253-3 dec just managed to beat the South 218-9 dec and 266 by a mere 10 runs. When the South second innings stood at 204-4 (Cox 82) victory seemed possible, but three brilliant catches turned the game. All through, every effort was made not to waste time, and for the last half hour played continued in heavy rain, with everyone determined to reach a finish. This was altogether a splendid start to the revival of Festival cricket with the interests of the spectators put first.

This was not the first time that an Indian team had appeared on the Central Ground since a pioneer team of Parsees had played there as long ago as 1886.

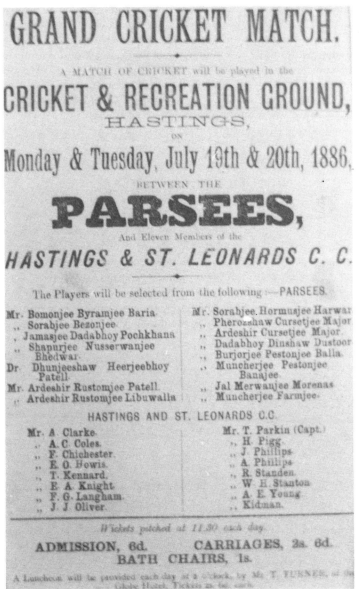

The pioneer team of Parsees play at Hastings in 1886.

The opening match of the 1947 Festival was dominated by expectations of Denis Compton breaking Jack Hobbs' 1925 record of scoring 16 hundreds in a season, as well as surpassing Tom Hayward's 1906 record aggregate of 3,518 runs in a summer. Both targets were achieved here in the course of two good matches reported now in some detail.

The South Africans v A South of England XI
3, 4, 5 September 1947

In the first game Denis Compton was playing for the South against visitors whose bowling he had treated mercilessly throughout the season, but now they were determined to make him fight all the way to break Hobbs' record. Before play began a black cat sauntered across the square, which was taken to augur well for Compton's chances. He started slowly, and there was a run-out scare with his score at 20, but he gradually speeded up, and at the tea interval he was on 97*. A glass of milk was all he wanted, and when play was resumed he blocked the first ball, but turned the second to the square-leg boundary in exactly the same direction as when he had equalled the Hobbs' record earlier that season. Now his score was 101 – his 17th century of the season, and the record was broken. The game was held up for 5 minutes whilst his team mates and a flock of cameramen flooded on to the field to join the rest in congratulations. When the excitement quietened down, Compton dashed down the wicket to the very next ball from Mann, the slow left-hander, and was comprehensively stumped. In the second innings he made 30, so the second target – of beating Hayward's aggregate record – was now reduced to 122.

I'm afraid the details of the rest of the game have become submerged in the high tide of Comptonitis, but the South Africans' first innings score of over 500 brought them eventual victory by 9 wickets.

Sir Pelham Warner's XI v South of England
6, 8, 9 September 1947

In reply to Warner's total of 306, the South were all out for 199. On a rain-affected pitch the side collapsed, and Compton going in later than usual was left high and dry with 87*. With more support this could have been his 18th century. It meant that in the second innings he now needed only 35 more runs to pass Hayward's total. He began cautiously against bowling that gave nothing away, but there was consternation among the huge crowd when he was dropped in the gully when he had made 22. At last Hayward's record was broken, and this time there was no question of throwing his wicket away, as there was a match to be won. He went steadily on to make 86 when he was bowled by Laker, who finished off the game with a hat-trick, and the South had lost by 26 runs.

92

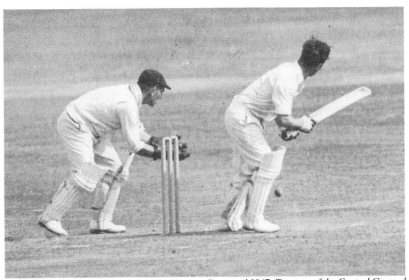

The stroke with which Compton broke Hayward's record 1947. Trustees of the Central Ground

Compton returns to applause after his innings.
Author's Collection

93

Though naturally elated by his record-breaking chiefly because his many runs had helped Middlesex to win the championship, Compton had no big ideas about records. He wrote: 'Records are made to be broken. I was just fortunate in the 1947 season, not only to strike my best form, but also to 'have the breaks'. I have no illusions about the latter. Things worked out extremely well for me.' His genius is not obscured by such endearing modesty.

As a post-script, Compton in his next and last innings of the season scored 246 for Middlesex against the Rest of England. He was totally carefree with no pressures on him, and though his knee was troubling him, he felt he could let himself go.

The Hastings Festival was privileged to be the scene of Compton's two record-breaking efforts, which I am certain will never be broken.

The Australians v The South of England
1, 2, 3 September 1948

The Australians came to Hastings determined not to lose their unbeaten record and they were greeted by a vast crowd.

Though S G Barnes was caught off the very first ball of the day, Bradman made the inevitable century (143), Hassett made 151, and in the evening Harvey made a superb 105*. The close of play score was 406-3, but not content with this, the Australians batted on next day until lunch time to take their total to 522-7 dec. The delayed declaration was possibly because a cold, sad drizzle was sweeping in from the sea, discouraging the idea of fielding. Harder rain later broke up the play. In the end the South reached 298 and that was the end. Compton was top scorer with 82 – yet another 80 score at Hastings – and he was presented by Sir Pelham Warner with a silver salver to commemorate his famous doings of the previous year. Though this was no great contest, we had seen Bradman honour the ground with a hundred, and (better still) we had seen Harvey at his best.

The West Indies v South of England   2, 4, 5 September 1950

The first ever visit of the West Indies enabled specators to see a fine 103 from C L Walcott, and 11 wickets taken by the wizard Ramadhin. In the first innings he bowled unchanged for 3 hours for figures of 7-67, but rain made it impossible to force a finish. In the second match – OVER 32 v UNDER 32 – there was an opportunity to see some promising newcomers such as J G Dewes, G H G Doggart, D B Carr, M F Tremlett, D Shackleton, R O Jenkins, and R Tattersall, but it was the 46-year-old Emrys Davies who took the honours with a score of 107* batting right through an innings of 180. In spite of this the youngsters won in the end by 6 wickets.

The Australians v South of England   2, 3, 4 September 1953

As usual the Australians put together a huge total, this time 564-9 dec, which was the biggest at Hastings since the Sussex record score of 705-8 d in 1902. The runs were made at a rate of 96 runs an hour, and the top scorers were Hassett 106, McDonald 125, de Courcy 118, and a dashing 85* from Davidson.

But the real high spot was Bill Johnston's effort of 5*. Before this his figures for the season were 14 matches, 15 innings, 14 not outs, 97 runs, 28* top score, average 97.00. He took a single, then hit a 4 to take his aggregate (and average) to 102, at which point Hassett promptly declared. In his next and last innings of the season he scored 0*, which left his average at 102.00. This was one of the best ever of cricket jokes, carefully plotted by Hassett.

South of England v The Rest   5, 7, 8 September 1953

The second match was a good contest. On the opening day The Rest made 300 in 4 hours, with Denis Brookes batting right through for 139*. The South replied with 307-5 dec (P E Richardson 56), and then The Rest had a disastrous start, losing 5 wickets for 41 to Shackleton and Perks, who always bowled well at Hastings. Fearing the game might end too soon, the regular bowlers were then taken off. George Tribe made the most of this opportunity, reached 103* in 75 minutes for the fastest hundred of the season, and went on to score 121 out of 182 in another 20 minutes. So the South now needed 227 to win. When the ninth wicket fell at 156 all seemed over, but the last pair, Laker and J A Young put on 43 in 15 minutes: this raised hopes of a dramatic victory, but Young fell at last, bowled by D V P Wright.

A Commonwealth XI v An England XI
1, 2, 3 September 1954

This game provided the almost perfect Festival finish, the Commonwealth XI winning by 22 runs with only 5 minutes to go. A side containing K M Archer, R E Marshall, F M Worrell, C L Walcott, B Dooland, V Mankad, G Tribe, B A Barnett, and S Ramadhin could not fail to play attractive cricket, but the side were all out for 261 to which the Rest replied with 236. The Commonwealth then scored 199-5 dec leaving the Rest 225 to win in 140 minutes. At the fall of the 4th wicket 87 runs were still needed in 55 minutes, but Dooland's leg-breaks, and Ramadhin's oddities were too much. Dooland not only scored 66 and 59, but also took 6 wickets. The match was a reminder of how many good overseas cricketers were summering in England, some of them playing in League cricket. This almost annual Commonwealth match provided a unique chance to see some very exciting players from overseas.

It was during the second match of the week – Pakistan v An England XI that I tried an experiment about the pace of bowling. With the support of the officials and of Gifford Boyd who kindly lent me a cine-camera, I took some pictures from the top of the old pavilion in a side-on position. The bowlers concerned were Trueman, Loader, Lock and Laker. The idea was to estimate their pace. Each frame in the film has a fixed time, and as it was possible to count the frames of each ball as it passed from wicket to wicket, a speed could be calculated. Very primitive no doubt compared with modern electronic devices, but it was at least a try. The results suggested that Trueman's recorded balls averaged 89mph, Loader's 70mph, Lock's 61mph, and Laker's 55mph.

I wish I could have filmed the ball with which Lock bowled Worrell at Hastings in the following year. It came down like a rocket, and Worrell, though well set, was left without a stroke. There was obviously something odd about it. This ball was one of the earliest of Lock's quicker balls which were later condemned as throws, and caused him to be no-balled. When he saw a film of these fast balls, Lock realised what was wrong, and immediately modified his action.

Sir Frank Worrell and George Tribe come out to bat in a Festival match in 1955.
John Hodges

96

A Commonwealth XI v An England XI
4, 5, 6 September 1957

This was an ideal game with the England XI winning by 3 wickets with only 7 minutes to go. After being behind on the first innings the Commonwealth, with 161 to the England XI's 277-5 dec, made up any deficit by scoring 366, of which the last 307 came in only 2½ hours. It was even scoring with P A Arnold's 77 the top score. The England XI were left with 281 to win in 2 hours 45 minutes. Colin Cowdrey, who had made 62 in the first innings, now made 100 in 90 minutes. He also managed to take 6 wickets in the match, his most successful bowling since his schooldays at Tonbridge. A few days before, he had scored 143 for L E G Ames XI against the West Indies, so he was the week's big hero. The Commonwealth XI included such interesting players as D G Phadkar and S P Gupte from India, J Pettiford and C G Pepper from Australia, and L Outschoorn from Ceylon.

A Commonwealth XI v An England XI
5, 7, 8 September 1959

This produced a good finish when the England XI won by 2 wickets with 263 needed to win. On batting first the Commonwealth lost 5 wickets for 86, but Alley 55 and Ibadulla 77 helped boost the score to 279. The side included R Subba Row, C L McCool, P M Walker, and B A Barnett, the Australian wicket-keeper who had toured here in 1938. He now lived in England, and frequently appeared at Hastings.

The England XI replied with 307-9 dec, D B Carr scoring 76 and J B Mortimore hitting 7 sixes in a score of 64. Subba Row and Outschoorn now put on 127 for the 1st wicket, and the Commonwealth reached 289. The England XI had a poor start, losing 3 of the first 5 wickets to Tribe, playing in his last match before returning to Australia. B Taylor of Essex then scored 56, and after the 8th wicket fell at 232, Mortimore 15* and N I Thomson 24* stayed together and knocked off the runs.

The Australians v A E R Gilligan's XI   2, 4, 5 September 1961

No previous festival had produced such sparkling batting. After the first two innings the Australians with 364 led the opposition by only 4 runs. On the first day no fewer than 563 runs were scored in 5½ hours (Gilligan's XI 360, Australians 203-4). Alley topscored with 102, Simpson made 65, O'Neill 81, Davidson 65, and Benaud 50 in 30 minutes. It was a run riot. Gilligan's side then scored 286, leaving the Australians 260 minutes to score 283 to win. The first hour produced 120 runs, Harvey made a dazzling 65 in 45 minutes, and Davidson another hard-hitting 60. The 283 runs were knocked off for the loss of 7 wickets in only 2 hours 45 minutes, with nearly 1½ hours to spare, but no one could complain about an early finish after seeing such joyful hitting.

A Commonwealth XI v An England XI
6, 7, 8 September 1961

It seemed difficult to match the hitting of the previous match, but this game was no anti-climax. The scores – Commonwealth XI 300 and 306 v An England XI 299 and 275 show how close it was, with the former winning by 41 runs. The highest scorers were Alley 82, Sobers 54 and 40, Jayasingh 88, and Hitchcock 55 and 54 for the Commonwealth, while for the England XI Alan Oakman made 116, which was a very popular event on his home ground. Titmus 60 and 64 supported him, while Subba Row in his retirement match was handsomely applauded for innings of 33 and 60. The bowlers had little success. However it was good to see such men as L Jackson of Derby, Lock and Loader of Surrey, the superb action of Wesley Hall, and Sobers taking 7 wickets with his all-sorts bowling. This was a week of which all could be proud.

The Australians v A E R Gilligan's XI   3, 4, 5 September 1964

This was the eighteenth visit of an Australian team to Hastings, but to quote *Wisden*: 'The cricket was too light-hearted at times to be treated seriously, but the crowd enjoyed plenty of entertainment.' Gilligan's XI scored 372 and 251-9 dec against the Australians' 281 and 346-8, which gave them a 2 wickets victory. This suggests a possible race against time, but the Australians won with 2 hours to spare. On the opening day Basil d'Oliveira in one of his earliest appearances in England made 119 with 4 sixes and 18 fours after Suttle and Barlow had put on 107 for the first wicket. For Australia O'Neill made a brilliant 74 and Cowper hit 14 fours in scoring 56. In Gilligan's second innings no fewer than 10 bowlers went into action, a miscellany much enjoyed by Norman 81 and Jim Parks 54. Grout the wicket-keeper took off his pads and got a wicket. The Australians had a tough target of 342 and were 63 for 1 at the end of the second day, but next morning Lawry made an unusually dashing 110, Booth made 69 and Cowper hit another 11 fours in scoring 56. It was a good win and no doubt the spectators had every reason to go home happy.

The absence of the New Zealand Touring team in 1965 was a sad blow to Festival plans, and in 1966 the West Indies had much of their game with A E R Gilligan's XI washed out by rain. Included in Gilligan's XI was a young South African qualifying for Sussex. His name was Tony Greig, and I remember a very tall shy young man looking rather lost at a reception in the Caves. The second part of the Festival in 1966 took the form of two one-day matches versus Kent and Surrey. This was the writing on the wall, and a sad come-down from the great days of the Hastings Festival. 1966 saw an end that came not 'with a bang but a whimper'. Festival cricket with all its memorable and happy traditions has never been seen again in Hastings.

Festival cricket for all its gaiety, always has a tinge of unhappy autumn feeling that the beloved season is coming to an end. The close of the 1966 festival at Hastings filled the spectators with an overwhelming melancholy.

5 · Some Recollections by Great Cricketers

The Central Ground Hastings has won praise from its very earliest days. In 1880 it was stated that among others W G GRACE regarded it as having 'the best and truest turf in the United Kingdom'. Many since then have declared it to be their favourite ground. In personal conversation and in print, MAURICE TATE said that Hastings was without doubt his favourite ground, and ARTHUR GILLIGAN in his book *Sussex Cricket* wrote:

'The Hastings ground is my favourite ground not only in Sussex but in the whole world. It may be because I have had a tremendous amount of success both in the batting and bowling line, but there never was a nicer playing area than Hastings.'

Now thanks to their fond memories of Hastings and their readiness to recall them as a tribute to the ground, I have assembled a team of great players who have provided me with the following recollections. These are presented in alphabetical order:

Leslie Ames   Kent (captain) and England

It is a sad thought that we will be deprived of seeing any more cricket on the Hastings Cricket Ground after the 1989 season. I have many pleasant memories of the ground, none more perhaps than my first glimpse of it. I was a boy of only 14 or 15 and was primarily on a church outing from the village where I lived in Kent. Upon arrival in Hastings I found Sussex were playing, and I think the opposition was Surrey. Father gave me and another boy the necessary admission money and off we went (entrance was 1s, boys 6d).

I always found the Hastings Ground and its people so homely. The Kent v Sussex games were always played at Hastings, and were of course being neighbouring counties, very much needle matches, but such was the rapport between the players there was a friendly understanding, especially with Chubby Tate, Ted Bowley, the Parks and Langridge brothers. The pitch in those days was one of the best and many high scores were to be made. One of the greatest innings I ever saw was Duleep's annihilation of Kent's great leg-break bowler Tich Freeman in 1929.

When the War broke out I was enlisted in the RAF and found my first posting was to the Marine Hotel, St Leonards, but only for a short time as we were all evacuated at the time of Dunkirk. I have a particular happy memory of two RAF games on the ground. In one game I didn't keep wicket, but bowled, taking nine wickets and catching the other. Although the standard was abyssmally low, it gave me a great deal of pleasure.

After the War and my retirement as a player I helped run the Hastings Cricket Festival for a number of years mainly by getting the players for the matches. Knowing the players personally helped greatly, so in spite of the popular festival at Scarborough I was able to get many of the top players to participate.

Surely the Hastings ground was unique in being literally right in the centre of the town, just a stroll from the seafront. Both before and after the War I played in many Kent/Sussex games at Hastings, and nothing can ever erase the many happy memories of the ground and the friendships made there.

Colin Cowdrey   Oxford University, Kent (captain), England (captain)

Kent cricketers always enjoyed playing at Hastings. A holiday crowd, the smell of the sea, the constant swirl and cry of the gulls, a firm natural pitch with pace and bounce, just the ingredients for a memorable day's cricket.

My first appearance on the ground was as a 19-year-old for Kent against Sussex in July 1951. David Clark was the Kent captain, but unable to play through injury and Jack Davies, in his place, lost the toss. John Langridge pushed the first ball of the match into the covers and set off for a quick single. Seeing Jack Davies swooping, and he was a magnificent fielder, John shouted at his partner, Don Smith, to go back but it was very late in the day. Kent fast bowler Freddie Ridgway had followed through a long way, and with Don Smith turning and starting to scamper back, Jack Davies had to throw the stumps down. Alas, he missed, and I can see the brand new shiny ball skimming across the brown outfield, across to the coach station, and clattering about on the asphalt of the car park.

It was a bad moment for us – the Sussex crowd beside themselves with excitement and the batsmen all smiles, Jack crestfallen, and the bowler not best pleased. But it was worth the gamble.

100

Ridgway then bowled beautifully and with great fire for an hour. Sussex were 160-7 mid-afternoon but David Sheppard, having survived early alarms, produced a magnificent hundred to save the day for Sussex. It was a memorable cricket. But it so often was at Hastings on this good, fast pitch and bowlers had to be at their very best to reap just rewards. Happy memories!

Ted Dexter Cambridge University (captain), Sussex (captain), England (captain)

Being in the right place at the right time is half the battle in life – and in cricket. The Priory Ground at Hastings was definitely the place to be for an aspiring England batsman on 20 July 1968, and I just happened to be the lucky man. An innings of some substance was needed if I was to justify the confidence of the then England captain, Colin Cowdrey, who had rung me up some weeks earlier to give warning of a possible recall to the colours. The England team was suffering a rash of injuries at the time. 'You would need to play a couple of county matches,' he told me, 'and hopefully make a few runs.'

Ted Dexter hits another boundary. Author's Collection

101

Derek Underwood

Robin Marlar, a fine off-spin bowler, and captain of Sussex 1955-59.
Sussex County Cricket Club

Now legend has it that Dexter made 203 on a nasty turner while all about him others failed. Admittedly things looked a little bleak, going in at 6 for 2 and losing 2 more partners, with only 27 scored. The pitch *was* turning sharply and Underwood had the ball.

I decided that counter-attack was my best ploy and had some success but, having gained a breather, it should be recorded that the damp pitch now dried out gently and gave bowlers little help from then on. Note that Kent made 289 in reply to 380 by Sussex.

My remaining memory of the match is prompted by an interview with Brian Johnston, given at the time when I remember making the bull point that I was still fit for big cricket despite playing only at weekends. But the day after, a nasty pain in my knee made itself felt and it never quite left me even during the 2 Test matches v Australia, which were my reward for all those runs v Kent.

Perhaps I wasn't quite so fit after all!

G Hubert G Doggart   Cambridge University (captain), Sussex (captain), England, President of MCC 1981-2

I share Gerald Brodribb's sadness that cricket will soon be a thing of the past on the Recreation Ground, whose coastal breezes and lively pitches regularly produced cricket in keeping with its seaside ambience.

The memories are vivid and my *Wisdens* ensure that I have not, like Homer, nodded. They start in 1948, when I first played for the county after the Cambridge term, and I was fortunate also to be picked to play in the Festival that year. To field to a Bradman hundred, and to be able to recount the story to one's grandchildren (when they arrive!) was bliss indeed.

It was at Hastings that dear Billy Griffith made one of his three hundreds – not to be compared with the one in Trinidad in 1948, when for the only time in his life he saw sweat actually come through the pads he was wearing, but something nonetheless to treasure. As I made exactly the same score in the next match – it was against Kent in 1949 – my recollection of Hastings is not unpleasurable.

There was the time, in 1950, that I tried in vain to persuade the West Indies to go for 122 in the final 55 minutes. Dear Sonny Ramadhin had earlier shown me his worn, Oh so worn, spinner finger, and I recalled with certain justifiable pride, that Cambridge had scored 504-3 in the day, off the full West Indian attack.

Finally, I remember John Flavell, of Worcestershire, taking the first nine Sussex wickets in 1954, and being kept on by Reg Perks for a last precious three-quarters of an hour while those stalwarts, Ted James and Jim Wood, had a stirring unbroken last-wicket partnership that paved the way for a great 9-wicket victory.

Yes, the Hastings ground had an atmosphere all its own, and I am not looking forward to my next visit. I suspect that I shall be tempted to 'create' something awful at what I see. Let us hope that the planners have not allowed that!

W H V (Hopper) Levett   Kent and England

I first saw cricket at Hastings in 1920 when a rather rotund Ranjitsinhji was playing his last match. I have nothing but pleasure from the memories of all the cricket I have played or witnessed there. The annual Kent v Sussex match was like a reunion of old friends, on such good terms were the players. The amateurs and professionals alike set the tone by playing as though they enjoyed every moment of the game and county cricket was a game then and not a business.

The Kent supporters crowded over the border by bus, train and car and with no drink-drive anxiety the beer tents became full of activity. The Saturday of the match always meant 'gates closed'.

I remember a reception at the Town Hall in 1948 when I was chatting with Bill Brown, Hassett and Bradman. Along came a prominent lady member of the council ready to make cricket conversation. She said: 'Oh, Mr Bradman, you must feel tired running over the field all day, chasing the ball?' Bradman, who had in fact been batting (he scored 143), and not fielding, replied with a twinkle that he did not feel too bad.

I remember once when some boys kept hitting a tennis ball on the field during the play and disturbing it. One of them was a very small Jim Parks, Jnr, and father Jim, who was on the field had to be called off to put a stop to his son's activities.

The closure of the ground saddens me greatly: there is no other ground with an atmosphere like the Central, Hastings: it was indeed the jewel in the crown of cricket.

Robin Marlar   Cambridge University (captain), and Sussex (captain)

Some thirty years ago Robin Marlar wrote 'one must have marvelled at the wisdom which gave Hastings its truly central ground', and he produces some recollections of his cricket there.

As a Sussex Young Amateur I used to come over to Hastings by bus from our farm at Mayfield and saw the great festival of 1947 and Bradman making his last century in England a year later. I think I played my first and last county game for Sussex at Hastings. We amateurs used to stay at the Queens Hotel and I recall David Sheppard trying to convert me through the connecting door of our suite. David was a magnificent player with huge confidence, and I can recall the look on the face of Jack Davies of Kent when David hit him on to the Chapel wall pretty high up.

We lost the championship in 1953 when our wicket-keeper, dear old soul, dropped Vic Wilson in the Yorkshire match, and that was it. That incident was the original prompt to get a better wicket-keeper, but none of the younger ones were much good, and this led, in the end, to Jim Parks being tried behind the stumps, and going on to keep wicket for England.

Another memory of the days of my comeback in 1968 is dropping Keith Fletcher with the easiest of 'caught and bowled', when he had made 99 – and he went on to score over 200.

I loved the old ground and I'm very sorry to see it go.

Alan Oakman   Sussex and England

In my very young days watching the following players representing the Priory were: Frank Watson, whom I tried to emulate as a bowler in the nets; Vic Pain, playing in a pair of crepe boots that I think he'd worn in the jungle during the War; Reg Robotham, a very prolific run scorer; Alf Coote, Manager of a local building society, who sat in judgment on everybody; dear Alf Dengate, a most tolerant and knowledgeable groundsman, who gave me a good deal of encouragement; Les Fuller, whom I used to bat against when he opened the bowling for the Hastings Police; Barry Funnell, who kindly lent me a bat and a cricket sweater when I played for Sussex Young Amateurs at Canterbury; and last, but by no means least, Bish Byrom, to whom I shall always be indebted, as it was he who was my Cricket Master at the Grammar School and did much to further my career.

I also remember playing for Sussex Young Amateurs against Yorkshire at Hastings and the team included David Sheppard and Ken Suttle. I can remember Jack Flavell of Worcestershire having taken nine wickets before lunch, and Hubert Doggart saying that if he couldn't get the last two batsmen out (they were A E James and D J Wood) then he shouldn't have all ten. Hubert gave him a quarter of an hour after lunch and then declared, the last two remaining undefeated in a last wicket stand of 55. Needless to say Flav was furious as they came off the field. I can remember Dexter scoring runs against Kent on a turning wicket and even the great Underwood came in for some punishment. I can remember Tommy Spencer, who played for Kent, batting for the British Legion when they played against the Hastings Priory. He was a marvellous cover point in those days. I remember Harry Preston, the groundsman, who had to have his hand amputated after catching it in the cutters of the mower. It happened in April while I was coaching there. I can still see him screaming in the distance and when we ran out to help him, his hand was wedged right up to the wrist and the engine still vibrating. As he lay crouching on his knees he said: 'Can you phone Mr — to tell him I shan't be able to coach his son tonight.' Amazing how the human mind and body works under stress!

106

I can remember working the scoreboard just after the war. The one near the dining room which just had tin plates and nails to hook on. In the last innings Surrey were chasing runs and I got in such a tangle trying to keep the total and each individual batsman's scores going that Dennis Hendren the umpire stopped the game and called across, telling me just to keep the total going.

I can remember Len Creese, who followed Harry Preston as groundsman – I can remember watching H E H Gabriel, with his bowling action – and Alan Grant who I felt could have gone on to better things had he had more opportunity.

It is indeed sad when I think of the Central Ground closing but I suppose there is good coming from this in as much as the Trustees will have better modern facilities and financial security. It will hopefully give the residents of Hastings a more varied selection of retail outlets and hopefully create more jobs in the town.

Paul Parker   Sussex (captain) and England

One of my first appearances at the Central Ground was in 1972 when I was scoring for Sussex II against Essex at the tender age of 16. The captain and the coach of the day was Les Lenham and the team were in dire straits on the last afternoon. At tea-time, Les urged the remaining batsmen to dig in for a draw. On the fall of our ninth wicket, out strolled a certain Dillip Doshi, who became India's main left-arm spinner in the latter half of the seventies. At this stage, he was famous in my eyes for having the largest wad of notes I'd ever seen when I came to collect up the valuables at the start of the day.

Les was the not-out batsman and could be heard from the boundary telling Dillip to get stuck in. The first ball was flighted up and Dillip played an immaculate forward defence. Loud encouragement and approval from the non-striker's end. The next delivery was again flighted up and our number eleven danced down the wicket and tried to hit the ball into the sea. He missed by a yard and was easily stumped.

The match was lost and Les followed Dillip into the pavilion, visibly angry and trembling with rage. While I was completing my scoring duties in the scorebox, an audible and unrepeatable row was taking place in the home dressing room. When peace had returned, I crept into the room to return the players' valuables. Les and Dillip were glaring at one another across the room. 'You'll never play in my side again!' Les was adamant. Mind you, so was Doshi. 'Mr Lenham, I have no desire to play for you again,' and with that, walked from the room. Half my mind was wondering if he would return to collect his fortune that was weighing down the valuables bag I was still carrying, but the other half was contemplating, with growing excitement, the prospect that the morrow

107

held. For Dillip Doshi's demise was my gain – I was to replace him against Glamorgan II on the following day, my first game for a senior Sussex side. (Dillip returned about five minutes later to collect his valuables.)

And this is how I shall remember the Central Ground – a ground of unusual occurences. Where else could one play a first-class match with the mist rising in mystical strands from the turf, where the ball scatters the massive herring gulls pecking at the grass, whose cries echo against the tall terraced buildings which overlook the arena? Where else could a ball be struck into the top deck of a passing bus? Ask Ken McEwan, the former Essex batsman.

A ground of unusual deeds and exciting cricket. Long will I remember the weekend a few years ago when we played Kent. On the Saturday, 21 wickets fell, with the advantage firmly in our favour. On Sunday, in the dreaded 40-over circus of the John Player League, Sussex were bundled off the park by Underwood, who came in as nightwatchman on that Saturday evening, and scored his only first-class hundred while the batsmen at the other end fell like a pack of cards. Indeed, at one stage the score was 110-7, with Underwood not out on 58. Nor was this the end of the tale, for Sussex, cantering to a win on the Tuesday needing 6 runs with four wickets in hand, were all out in the next two overs with scores level. A tie – but somehow, this result seemed inevitable.

The following year I wondered if the heroics of the recent past would be repeated. Our game against Northamptonshire was well in our favour and, with the wicket behaving erratically and dangerously, the opposition required 320 to win on the last day. That morning the Test team was announced and the twelve included Wayne Larkins, who was opening their innings and averaging below 15 that season. A wicked delivery from Imran broke the opener's hand early in the innings and the stage was set for an early Sussex victory. Enter Allan Lamb who had been overlooked by the England selectors on the same morning. There proceeded a battery of vicious and thrilling shots from Lamb who amassed 150 in very quick time and put Northants on the trail of an unlikely victory. Even so, the last pair had to put on 20 in a very tense final session before we finally succumbed. It was an amazing reversal of fortune but typical of the essential nature of the Central Ground.

And those who had written off the County last season when we were bowled out by Kent for 71 on the first morning, should have paid more heed to recent history. For we came within an ace of beating our great rivals and the game went right into the last over of the match.

I have enjoyed my cricket at the Central Ground and will miss its unique atmosphere.

108

Jim Parks Sussex (captain) and England

How sad to see the end of cricket on the Central Ground. I say this with much conviction, although there were times in the 60s when I used to dread the Hastings Week.

During that period, after Len Creese had left and gone to Hove as groundsman at the County Ground, the wicket slowly deteriorated until batting became an absolute nightmare, and invariably it was the destroyer Derek Underwood who had a field day. Derek did in fact let it be known that he would have liked to dig the Hastings wicket up and take it with him. Perhaps at the end of September he might be allowed to do so.

I first played at Hastings in 1947 as a member of the Sussex Young Amateurs, as the young hopefuls were called in those early days after the war, and I remember well getting some turn from my leg spinners.

It was in 1952 before I was at the Central Ground with the Sussex side. I happily managed to get a century against Surrey on that occasion, which of course means that I shall always have fond memories of my associations with Hastings.

Other innings stand out in my mind: Ted Dexter came out of retirement to help the team in 1968 and scored one of the finest double centuries I have seen, with Derek Underwood very much in the back seat on that occasion. I was privileged to be captain of Arthur Gilligan's XI in the Festival of 1968 when we saw Basil D'Oliveira score his maiden first-class hundred in this country. Basil was still qualifying for Worcester at the time and gave us all an insight of things to come.

Happy memories, all of them, some more vivid than others, but certainly all of us that enjoyed playing on the Central Ground will regret its passing, and I wonder whether ghosts of players past will haunt the shopping precinct in years to come when the time arrives for the Hastings Week?

David Sheppard The Right Reverend Bishop of Liverpool
Cambridge University (captain), Sussex (captain),
England (captain)

In his book *Parson's Pitch* (1964), David Sheppard recalls his first appearance for Sussex as an eighteen-year old in 1947. With his permission I quote the passage here:

'My first county match was against Leicestershire at Hastings. "They're not a very strong bowling side," I was told. "The only bowler you really want to worry about is Jack Walsh. He bowls one googly you can see, and one googly you can't see." I said I would look out for Walsh. "Then be careful with Watson in the field, because he can throw with either hand." I said I would keep my eyes open for Watson. Unfortunately the only ball I had in the first innings was from Jackson, and they hadn't told me about him. It was a little in-swinger that nipped in and trapped me leg before wicket – out first ball.

'In the second innings I did a little better and at the tea interval on the third day I was 0 not out. As we went on the field after tea, Les Berry, the Leicestershire captain, said, "There'll be a run for you on the off-side if you want it." I said, "Thank you very much." All the fielders went back a few yards so that I could push an easy single. I did this – and I got one more run without any help. I then was caught at the wicket off Lester for two. And I still hadn't had a ball from Walsh, or recognised which one was Watson.

'That evening we set off by coach from Hastings, with its boarding houses sending their smell of fried fish across the pleasant, enclosed ground, making the fieldsman long for his lunch long before the interval comes at 1.30pm.'

I had first met David Sheppard when he was captaining the Sherborne colts against my colts side at Canford school. I was sitting with the family at his debut match, and next day after this sad duck, in order to cheer David up I produced a list I had found of Great Batsmen who had opened their first-class career with a duck. There were many including Grace, Hammond and Hutton. Little did we realise then that the Sheppard name would also later qualify to be among the great.

Derek Underwood   Kent and England

He has kindly allowed the reproduction of this piece from his 1986 Benefit Brochure:

My first appearance on a first-class cricket ground occurred on 7 June 1960, and yes, it was on the Central Ground, Hastings. This, in itself, is enough to give special meaning, but little did I know that this ground would prove to be such a happy hunting ground in years to come. On my first county appearance there in 1963 I suffered at the hands of Messrs Dexter, Parks and Suttle, all of whom scored hundreds and I came out of the match with figures of one wicket for 94 runs. I wasn't so keen on Hastings then!

1964 saw a complete change of fortune and a dry, dusty wicket, just tailor-made for me, gave me an opportunity to take some wickets in the second innings. 9 for 28 was the result, which has remained my best bowling performance, figuratively, ever since. Incidentally, two weeks earlier against the same opposition, I had finished with 1 for 120 at Tunbridge Wells.

1967: Again fortune was to shine on me with Kent batting the first day with torrential rain following overnight, and a drying wicket to bowl on next day. 7 for 38 1st innings followed by 7 for 44 in the 2nd. This remains my highest wicket tally in a match in this country.

1968: This was a different story as Ted Dexter returned from a 2 year absence from the first class game and he proceeded to score a mammoth 203 out of 313, racing to his second hundred in just over 1½ hours. 4 for 144 from 42 overs, was my tally and a tired and weary individual I was too!

1973: Kent scored 282 on the Wednesday and again rain overnight and a hot sun the next morning produced ideal conditions for me. 5 for 43 in the first innings and 8 for 9 in the second, the Kent players having spent considerable time mopping up. This was Tony Greig's first match as captain of Sussex and afterwards he vowed that Kent would never play again at Hastings – a long time was to elapse.

1985: 1 July, Sunday League. A 12-year lapse and a return to Hastings. On this occasion, thanks to 3 brilliant stumpings by Knotty, I finished with 6 for 12 from my 8 overs, my best return in a John Player League Game. A very kind Sussex supporter sent me a video of the whole match, which naturally I treasure greatly.

2 July saw me continue my night watchman role and scrape through to my maiden hundred. I believe there is only one other player who played more innings than me before finally scoring a hundred, that player being Bob Taylor. It took me 618 innings in first class cricket to reach that goal. I think there is a moral there somewhere. If at first you don't succeed, try, try again! I shall always remember the support I received from Terry Alderman at the other end, and the relief of Kevin Jarvis, who was next in. Incidentally, this match was a tie, the first in county cricket for 11 years.

So, to summarise, Hastings has seen my Best Bowling performance in an innings, my Best Match performance in this country, my Best Sunday League Bowling performance, and now, of all things, my Highest Score. No wonder I have fond memories of Hastings.

6 · Famous Local Cricketers

Throughout the history of cricket there have been many famous brotherhoods, such as the Graces, Fosters, Walkers, Lytteltons and Chappells, but no county exceeds Sussex with such a record as the Gilligans, Parks, Langridges, Oakes, Busses, Greigs and Wells. From Hastings there was one set of brothers – the six Phillips brothers – who had much to do with the raising of the standard of local cricket. In 1874 five of them played for Hastings against The East Sussex Club on the old racecourse at St Leonards, and together they provided 174 runs out of the side's total of 241. The six brothers in order of age were, Albert, William, Henry, James, Peter and Fred. The achievements of three of them are recorded here.

HENRY PHILLIPS

(Better known as Harry) was born at Hastings on 14 October 1844 and spent all his life in the town, until his death in 1919. He first appeared for Sussex as a long-stop in 1868, and made his debut as a wicket-keeper in 1870 when he stumped 4 and caught 1 of Surrey at the Oval: he remained the Sussex 'keeper for the next 20 years. He wrote that as a boy he used to long-stop as often as he could in early morning practices at the top of the East Hill near the Castle. Though his height of only 5ft 4in might have seemed a handicap in the days when rough wickets made the ball lift head high, he was extremely nimble, long-armed and ambidextrous. On one occasion he took a wide catch in his left hand from a firm glance off one of Southerton's leg-side deliveries. His speed enabled him to get to balls popped up on the leg-side, and in the 1871 Gentlemen v Players match at Hove he ran well past square-leg to take a catch that put an end to W G Grace's big score of 217. His agility enabled him at times to dispense with a long-stop. It is often claimed that he was the first wicket-keeper to do so, the chief evidence being a report of the Sussex v Gloucestershire match in 1873 which stated: 'Phillips kept wicket so good that he used no long-stop.' Remember too that in those days wicket-keepers' gloves gave little protection. His gloves, to be seen in the Pavilion at Hove, seem little more than gardening gloves. But he was very courageous. In the first game in which he played under Sussex auspices he was asked to keep wicket for the Gentlemen of Sussex against the Colts. He soon broke a finger, but stayed on the field and that evening obtained a thick piece of india rubber tubing to wear next day.

The *Sheffield Telegraph*, reporting the match between Sussex and Yorkshire in 1874, wrote: 'Phillips' dexterity was something marvellous as wicket-keeper and his side rightly put faith in his ability.' A lively wicket-keeper makes all the difference to the enthusiasm of the whole team. In one match however, his team was to be disappointed. When Sussex met Notts in 1873 they were all out for 19 and the scorebook has the unusual entry: 'Phillips . . . absent, missed the train . . . 0'.

His most important game was when he was chosen for the Players v The Gentlemen at Lord's in 1873 – the biggest match of the year. He was at one time offered an engagement on the Lord's staff, but refused it owing to his business interests, which included being a cabinet maker. His most dramatic success was against Surrey at the Oval in 1872 for he had 10 victims in the match – 5 ct and 5 st. As the Surrey wicket-keeper, Pooley, also had 5 wickets, the two keepers captured as many as 15 wickets of the 32 that fell. In 1884 v Kent, Phillips took 8 wickets – 5ct and 3 st.

Harry Phillips. Author's Collection

Occasionally, he used to go on to bowl some unusual left-handed lobs, keeping his pads on. He had little pretensions as a batsman, and easily his greatest innings was that against the Australians at Hove in 1884. On the day after England had just defeated the visitors by an innings, Sussex batted first, but thanks to the efforts of Giffen, Palmer, Boyle and Spofforth, 7 wickets had fallen for only 191 when Phillips, at No. 9, came in to join the amateur G N Wyatt. These two put on 182 for the 8th wicket before Wyatt was out for 112, with the total now 373. When stumps were drawn Phillips' score was 109* and he was chaired off the field by spectators 'in a scene of excitement scarcely equalled on a cricket field'.

An instant collection of 21 guineas was made for him – a good sum in those days. No one was more surprised at his success than Phillips himself: apart from a chance in the slips, when he had made 95, he had batted faultlessly, but he added only 2 more runs next day.

When the Hastings Festival was started in 1887 he took much interest in it, and in 1891 he played his final first-class match, on his much-loved home ground. He caught out Grace, Stoddart, Read and C A Smith in that Gentlemen v Players match. It is interesting to note that H R Butt, who became Phillips' successor in the Sussex team, played for the Hastings Alexandra Club in 1889, and died at Hastings in 1928.

In the 1870s there happened to be five great wicket-keepers whose names all began with the letter P – Plumb, Pinder, Pooley, Pilling and Phillips. Though the others may have gained more representative honours, none surpassed Phillips for energy and pluck. To quote *Wisden*: 'He was always the cheeriest of cricketers. No day was long enough to dampen his spirits.'

JAMES PHILLIPS

James was five years younger than Henry, and from early days showed great promise, WG himself speaking highly of him. In 1871 he played for the Colts of Sussex against the Sussex XI on the old Brunswick ground and made a masterly score of 103. Critics regarded this innings as the best Colts innings they had ever seen. James was promptly drafted into the county side, and opening the innings against Kent scored 37 before being bowled by 'Farmer' Bennett. As a result of this innings the Surrey executive invited him to play in a great match at the Oval the following week for Players of the South v the Gentlemen of the South. In a high scoring match the Players won by 3 runs, only 10 minutes before time. James was twice cheaply dismissed by the fast underhand grubs of C I Thornton, the biggest hitter ever. He played for Sussex in 3 games in 1871, but did not appear for the county at all in 1872-3. Next year however, saw him well established in the side. To quote *Wisden*: 'James Phillips has deservedly won high praise from all classes of critics for since 1864 no Colt has played the game with such truth, skill and patience: he was not ciphered once, and of his 16 innings, 13 were doubles.' In the same year, when playing for the United South against the United North at Wellingborough, he scored 19 and 19* and his fielding was 'especially commended'.

Owing to his business commitments James played only intermittently for Sussex over the next few years, but in 1878 played enough to top the Sussex averages, including a magnificent innings of 77* out of a total of 145 v Gloucestershire at Cheltenham. A week or so later he played for the English professionals against the Australians at the Oval and was top scorer in each innings.

Though his first-class appearances were much curtailed by his business as a tax accountant and Relieving officer, he had time to play a great deal of local cricket. Between 1870 and 1885 he had an average of 35 and scored 7 centuries for the Hastings Club. Such an average was very high for those times. He became the first secretary of the Club when it was reformed in 1873, and did much to help with the Festival and appeared in the opening week of 1887. In 1894 he wrote a booklet called *A review of Local cricket with special reference to the Hastings and St Leonards cricket Club*. He died 10 years later.

ALBERT PHILLIPS

Albert Phillips made his mark on Hastings cricket when on 9 June 1864, while playing for Hastings United against Northiam at Northiam, he became the first player ever to reach a century in the neighbourhood of Hastings. In the Club's second innings of 229 he batted right through to score 127*. In the return match, played on the East Hill, Albert 'greatly distinguished himself' by scoring the first century ever made at Hastings, a score of 104* in an innings total of 169. In a local review of cricket in 1880, a report says: 'Albert, in our opinion the best and prettiest bat among the brothers, has more than once been solicited to play for Sussex, and it is a matter of regret that his name has not figured in the county team, of which he would undoubtedly have proved one of the safest and reliable batsmen.'

EDWARD J McCORMICK

Born in Hastings in 1862, he played in 46 matches for the county as an all-rounder before his career as a banker curtailed his cricket. His most famous success was at Hastings in the Festival of 1889. When the Gentlemen needed 75 to win, it was only thanks to his innings of 25* that they won by 1 wicket.

Another Hastings worthy was **HERBERT PIGG** (1856-91) who played regularly in the Festival. Though he never played for Sussex, he had been a Cambridge Blue, and later played for Northants. In the Gentlemen v Players match of 1889 he had analyses of 4-57 and 7-55, and when playing for the South of England v the Australians in 1886, he scored 59 runs and took 8 wickets. One of the finest innings ever seen at Hastings was his 180 against the Yorkshire county XI in 1887, described elsewhere. He had a cricketing brother called Charles, and they were known as Hot and Cold Pigg.

Other local players from the Hastings area included: **G K PAPILLON** who played for the Gentlemen in the 1892 Festival: he lived at Crowhurst Park and the Papillon family were related by marriage to the Rev **HENRY CHARLES LENOX TINDALL**, who played in the Festival in 1893-4 and also three times for Kent. At Cambridge he was better known as an athlete and won the 440 yards Amateur Championship in 1889.

Another keen supporter of Hastings cricket was **H M CURTEIS** of Windmill Hill, Hailsham. He had been an Oxford Blue, and played 43 times for Sussex. He became MP for Rye. Perhaps better known as an administrator than a player was **THOMAS PARKIN**, who had much to do with the development of cricket at Hastings. He kept many interesting scrap books with local scores and reports. He wrote the section on Hastings cricket in Vol II of the *Victoria County History* (1907).

Few cricketers have made a more dramatic debut into first-class cricket than **JACK W W NASON** in the county match v Warwickshire in 1906. E W Dwyer, the Sussex fast bowler, after sending down only 5 overs, damaged a finger so badly that he could take no further part in the game. Nason, a local teenager, was watching the game and was invited to field as substitute and later on the Warwickshire captain generously (but illegally) allowed him to bat for Sussex in place of Dwyer. Nason made only 4 in the first innings, but when the county followed on, 178 runs behind, he hit out freely to become top scorer with 53*. He was barely seventeen, and was highly applauded. He later won a Cambridge Blue, played 22 games for Sussex and 19 more for Gloucester, only to be killed in the war in 1916.

In 1925 **A L NEWBERY** from Battle played three games for Sussex and later became manager of Gray-Nicholls bat-factory at Robertsbridge. Another contemporary at Hastings was **ALAN L WISDEN**, descendant of the famous John Wisden. He was an outstanding local cricketer, quite good enough to have taken part in county cricket. Another player from Battle, **ROBERT G STAINTON**, was an Oxford Blue who made his debut for Sussex in 1936 and played 72 innings for Sussex at an average of 24. He was a stylish batsman and fleet-footed fielder. He was Headmaster of Glengorse School for many years.

In the 1930s one outstanding batsman was **TOM W SPENCER**; he was considered for the county, but later joined Kent and played in 76 matches for them. I can well remember one game at Hastings in which I played when Spencer hit 7 balls out of the ground. In 1950 he joined the umpires' list and stood in 17 Test matches. Another fine Hastings batsman of the same time was **REG ROBOTHAM**. He played once for Sussex v MCC in 1946 and, but for the war, might well have made a name in county cricket.

The most famous name among Hastings-born cricketers must surely be **ALAN S M OAKMAN**. He played nearly 500 games for the county, scored 21,800 runs and took 736 wickets with his slow off-breaks delivered from his great height. He hit 1,000 runs in a season 9 times and 2,000 twice. His highest score was 229* v Notts at Trent Bridge in 1961. He twice played for England including the famous Laker match at Old Trafford in 1956: he also toured S Africa with MCC in 1956-7. On his

116

retirement in 1968 he took an appointment as coach with Warwickshire and is now assistant secretary there. The story of his introduction to cricket is worth telling. He first set foot on the Central Ground as a boy of 14, and was promptly hit on the ankle by a ball hit from the nets. In spite of this he went again to the ground a few weeks later, and this time stood behind the nets. He watched the batsman with increasing interest, and began to think: 'If he can do that, so can I'. He had never yet held a cricket bat or bowled a ball, but thanks to encouragement at the Grammar School, and his own natural ability, he was playing for Sussex by the age of 17 – only three years later – an incredible story. What other England player has never played any cricket at the age of fourteen!

The story of the Priory cricket club has already been told. One of their leading batsmen was **TIM D BOOTH JONES**, who was so successful that in 1980 he accepted an offer from the Sussex CCC to join the staff. Next year he made 95 against Somerset, his topscore in 26 matches for Sussex before returning to Club cricket and his teaching. It is not often that a good club cricketer – at the age of 28 – can step easily into the county game, but his experience proves that there must be many club players good enough to make a name in county cricket, but for circumstances (or inclination) that have prevented this.

Any survey of cricket in Hastings must include reference to **ARTHUR HAYGARTH** who was born at 29 Wellington Square in 1852. Though he was an accomplished cricketer he is best known as editor and compiler of the MCC *Scores and Biographies*. He wrote much on the game and in important matches at Lords often showed courageous defence. When asked what his average was, he would reply 'One hour', since he valued the occupation of the wicket almost as highly as runs.

Another cricket writer of a different kind was **G D MARTINEAU** whose home was at Martineau Lodge, in Martineau Lane. He wrote several scholarly and graceful books such as *The Field is full of Shades* and *Bat, Ball, Wicket and All*, and many articles chiefly concerned with the early days of cricket. His delight in the game began with watching big matches at Hastings, and as a boy he was lucky enough to witness Jessop's historic 191 in 1907.

7 · Some Historic Hits

'The Big Hit for six is the most companionable of cricketing acts'.

John Arlott

There is no doubt that the spectacular hit is remembered by those who saw it long after many a century or hat-trick is forgotten. The sight of the soaring ball is imprinted with joy upon the lens of memory.

Here is a survey of the memorable hits made at Hastings. The compact Central ground invites big hitting for the boundaries are short and there is little space between the boundary line and the wall surrounding the ground. A straight hit of 100 yards from either end can land the ball into Station Road or South Terrace. A hit to leg from the sea-end wicket needs a carry of 85 yards to land on the raised gardens of the houses in Devonshire Road behind the old Pavilion; before the Coote stand was built in 1959 the wall along Queens Road was 110 yards from a centrally-placed pitch.

It is not surprising that there have been many famous hitting feats. One of the best came in the very first match ever played on the new ground on August 29, 30, 31 1864; the United All England XI were playing XXII of Hastings and St Leonards. The United team included some of the best players in England; in their second innings of 129 they were saved from disaster by a dashing score of 60 by George Griffith, better known as Ben or 'the Lion'. He was a left-hander and was facing the skilful bowling of 'Farmer' Bennett, a slow left-handed bowler from the Kent side, who was 'given man' for Hastings. Here is an account of Griffith's innings:

'Griffith at the northern wicket with one of his tremendous hard hits sent the ball clean over the Goods Station Road. The whole of the over of Bennett's slows – 4 balls in succession – were struck to the same spot, to the dismay of the bowler, but to the increasing joy of the lookers-on, who were in a state of high excitement at such an unprecedented circumstance. General and oft-repeated applause showed the warmth of feeling that existed. Each ball counted 6 as "lost", so that 24 runs were made in a single over. The hat was sent round and a handsome sum was subscribed for the hero of the match.'

Another report says that the hits were all on-drives carrying some 115 yards, and one eye-witness wrote: 'I saw the feat as a lad. Each hit went over Station Road into Middle Street, and what is more the same house was hit each time. I shall never forget it. 'Seeing is believing', and I am sure of my facts.' The last ball of the over provided the biggest hit when Griffith ran halfway down the pitch to meet it, and the ball landed on the roof of a house.

This feat of four consecutive sixes was repeated by A W Greig when scoring 226 v Warwickshire in 1975. He was batting at the South Terrace end, had just reached his 200 and was facing the off-breaks of P J Lewington. The four sixes all went to square leg, and one was the biggest leg hit I have ever seen. It landed on the small pent-house roof of the Alfred Coote stand, and bounced into Queens Road – almost clearing the stand. The line of the shop fronts is 110 yards from the wicket, and the roof was 31ft high. It was a huge hit. Greig was going for a fifth – threatening perhaps to equal Sobers' record – but he skied the ball to a great height only to be well caught by Amiss on the very edge of the long-on boundary.

In the 1920s before the new stand was built Tate is said to have been the only batsman to hit a ball into Queens Road, and in 1966 D W Allan, in his score of 51, made a square leg that ended up in the road. Few others have been able to land the ball even as far as the top seating. Another huge leg hit more in the direction of wide mid-on was a drive by Jessop in his innings of 191 in 1907: this went right over the entrance gates in Queens Road and hit the window of the shop on the corner across the road from the Cannon Cinema (the old Gaiety Theatre).

Several players have put the ball on the roof of the old magistrates' court attached to the Town Hall: these include Grace, Ranji, Lord Tennyson, Watt, Dexter and Tate. In 1904 the giant South African J H Sinclair in scoring 27 made an on-drive that is said to have run 'almost to the Queens Hotel', and he also hit a ball that nearly killed his newly-wedded wife. Another of his hits in the same innings put a ball through the first-floor window of a house that stands on the corner facing the south entrance of the old bus station. This must have had a carry of at least 125 yards, and may be the hit in which the lady of the house refused to return the ball until some money was given to her for the repair of the window.

Straight hits have frequently cleared the Station Road wall, and reached the face of the houses 114 yards from the far wicket. In 1888 W W Read, in scoring 96 for the South v the North, hit a ball from Peel on to a roof and the ball ended up in a gutter. A man got a ladder and retrieved the ball 'amid thunderous applause'. This hit was claimed as THE HIT OF THE WEEK. Two years later Read made a similar hit which went into the first-floor window of a hotel where people were having tea. The drawn blinds saved them from injury, and they appeared at the window, smiling and waving their handkerchiefs. In 1906 P A Perrin in his 150 for Essex landed a ball on the roof of a house, and in 1938 Alan Watt put one right over a house into the back garden.

Station Road has never been so heavily bombarded since Robert Relf, in scoring 97 for the Players v the Gentlemen in 1909, hit one six off McDonnell into South Terrace, and then two more sixes off him into Station Road. He also repeatedly hit the ball to land high up on the wall.

He would certainly have reached his century if six had then been given for hits over the boundary line. In 1924 Relf displayed more 'tremendous hitting' with 7 sixes in his innings of 114 in 75 minutes against Lord Cowdray's XI.

Consider now big hits made from the sea-end wicket. To the leg-side are the gardens of the houses in Devonshire Road – a natural grandstand crowded with deck-chairs. The retaining wall behind the old Pavilion is only 85 yards from the centre, but as the gardens are on raised ground it requires a good hit to land the ball there, and is a rare hit. In 1910 Robert Relf (again) in scoring 31 v Kent swept a ball from Blythe into the gardens in a long-leg direction. In the previous year F E Woolley (left-handed) made a similar hit when batting at the South Terrace end; others known to have reached the gardens include Tate off Fender in 1933 and C Smart off Wensley in 1935. Tate wrote of the 1935 week: 'Never since I have been playing for Sussex have I seen so many sixes at the Central Ground. Some were tremendous swipes'.

One of the these swipes was made by George Pearce, the deaf butcher from Horsham, who on-drove a ball from Mercer to land on the roof of the brand new Pavilion in the north west corner of the ground. This was a good carry, but an even bigger hit clearing the Pavilion altogether was a drive by David Sheppard in his great score of 181* in 1953.

To a batsman at the sea-end a drive into South Terrace is as tempting as a drive into Station Road from the other end: the wall is 96 yards away, and the front of the house across the road is 112 yards away. The windows of the Friends Meeting House and the Free Christian Church (built in 1867) were said to have been an attraction for Jessop, and others too have broken windows. D L A Jephson tells a good story about K S Ranjitsinhji. In the match between the South of England and the Australians in 1899 someone reminded Ranji that he had never hit a ball out of the ground at Hastings. Ranji pondered a moment and then said: 'Let me stay in 30 minutes and I'll put one through that round window in the church over there'. Some 20 minutes later came the crash of glass as a ball delivered by Trumble arrived at its chosen destination.

The roofs of the houses are irregular, with some rising to four storeys, and I doubt if anyone has ever landed a ball as high as on the roof, but Woolley in 1923 once on-drove a ball from Tate which smashed the coping almost at roof level of the Cricketers' Hotel, and in 1953 the Australian, Alan Davidson, in his 85* drove a ball to the upper levels of the Friends Meeting House, a blow said by Jack Fingleton to be one of the biggest sixes ever seen on the ground. The mark is still visible. Another good hit in that direction was made by S Bartels, a Lancashire League player appearing for the Commonwealth XI in 1958. After thumping the ball and losing it in the unfinished shop buildings on the Queens Road frontage, from the other end he then made a beautiful straight drive 'that soared like a lark' out of the ground and landed through an open window of an upper storey room in South Terrace. This ball was also temporarily lost, but some time later was found tucked up in the curtains. Jack Oakes is another who landed a ball very high up on the face of a house in a drive off Dovey of Kent in 1950.

All these drives must have had potentially very long carries in hitting a building 112 yards at some 40 or so feet up. One of the earliest of these hits was made by W Bates in scoring 61 for the North v the South in 1886 when he drove a ball from G A Lohmann high against the Free Christian Church, described as 'one of the best hits seen on a cricket field for a long time'. Another well-remembered hit into South Terrace was one of the sixes off Freeman in Duleep's famous 246 in 1929. It cleared the Members' stand easily and crashed through a window in the Princes Hotel.

It is a pity that long hits cannot be more accurately measured, but I am sure some of those mentioned here could have been up in the 150 yards class. More important, each one provided for the spectators a very happy memory. It is surely right that such hits should be recorded for posterity:

> Yet even from the pedant what a deep ecstatic sigh
> When the batsman jumps to meet one and a sixer climbs the sky.
>
> E V Lucas

Here are some of the best six-hitting feats:

8 sixes	F M Worrell	101	A E R Gilligan's XI	v	N Zealand	1958
7	R Relf	114	The Rest	v	Lord Cowdray's XI	1924
7	J B Mortimore	64	England XI	v	Commonwealth XI	1959
6	C C Smart	151	Glamorgan	v	Sussex	1935
6	C G Smith	79	West Indies	v	L E G Ames XI	1957
6	A W Greig	226	Sussex	v	Warwickshire	1975

A spree of sixes from Worrell and Sobers v N. Zealand 1958. Trustees of the Central Ground

121

Consecutive sixes

4	(6666w)	A W Greig	226	Sussex	v	Warwickshire	1975
		(off P J Lewington)					
3	(1246660)	J C Clay	35	Glamorgan	v	Sussex	1937
		(off Jas Langridge)					
3	(6661..)	J B Mortimore	64	England XI	v	Commonwealth	1959
		(off J S Manning)					

3 sixes in 4 balls: A Buss 37 off A L Dixon Sussex v Kent 1967

In the course of the match between A E R Gilligan's XI and New Zealand in 1958 16 sixes were hit, 14 of them on the third day.

Runs off an over

26   644444   G L Jessop   off A E Relf   Gentlemen v Players   1907
24 runs have been achieved by J C Clay and A W Greig (see above)

8 · Facts and Figures and a Few Extras

First-class cricket at Hastings 1865-1988

Highest Totals

705-8 dec	Sussex	v	Surrey	1902
564-9 dec	Australians	v	South of England	1953
560-9 dec	Sussex	v	Kent	1930
554	Sussex	v	Kent	1936

There have been 9 other totals of over 500.

The highest match aggregates have been:
– 1427 for 21 wickets in Sussex v Surrey match in 1902: this was at the time the record aggregate for a match in England.
– 1451 for 36 wickets in Sussex v Kent match in 1929; this is the second highest aggregate for a county championship match.

Lowest Totals

54	Kent	v	Sussex	1972
54	Sussex	v	Kent	1973
56	Sussex	v	Derbyshire	1963
59	Gentlemen	v	Players	1901

There have been 9 other totals of under 70. The lowest match aggregate for one side is 121: Sussex 67 and 54 v Kent 1973.

Highest Individual Scores

246	K S Duleepsinhji	Sussex	v	Kent	1929
234*	K S Ranjitsinhji	Sussex	v	Surrey	1902
228*	K W R Fletcher	Essex	v	Sussex	1968
226	A W Greig	Sussex	v	Warwickshire	1975
218	G H Hirst	Yorkshire	v	Sussex	1911
203	E R Dexter	Sussex	v	Kent	1968
202	J Vine	Sussex	v	Northants	1920
202	Jn Langridge	Sussex	v	Leicester	1939

The highest score in a non-county match is G L Jessop's 191 v Players of the South in 1907.

Two Hundreds in a Match have been scored by J T Tyldesley (1900), K S Duleepsinhji (1929), and G D Mendis (1985).

Carrying Bat Right Through the Innings by W Rhodes (1923); C N Woolley (1925); E H Bowley (1926); E Davies (1950); D Brookes (1953) and N H Rogers (1954).

High-Scoring Stands: 279-3rd wkt D S Sheppard 181* and C Cox 144, Sussex v Yorkshire 1953; 266-3rd wkt R Aird 113 and C P Mead 154, Hants v Sussex 1924; 259-4th wkt G H Hirst 218 and A Drake 115, Yorks v Sussex 1911; 254-6th wkt C E de Trafford 110 and E Smith 154, North v South 1893.

There have been 15 other stands of over 200.

Century Makers: 205 centuries have been made. The most frequent scorers have been G L Jessop 6; F E Woolley, J H Parks, Jn Langridge and A E Fagg 5 each; K S Duleepsinhji, H W Parks, Jas Langridge, L E G Ames, D S Sheppard, K G Suttle and J M Parks 4 each.

Bowling Records

9 wickets in an innings:

9-83	E J Tyler	Somerset	v	Sussex	1907
9-87	A P Freeman	Kent	v	Sussex (300-9 d)	1921
9-55	J A Young	England XI	v	Commonwealth	1951
9-122	J A Flavell	Worcester	v	Sussex (307-9 d)	1954
9-28	D Underwood	Kent	v	Sussex	1964

8 wickets in an innings have been taken by:
S M J Woods (1892); J T Hearne (1896); T Richardson (1898); P R May
(1907); A E Relf (1908); F E Woolley (1910); G Cox (1912);W C Smith
(1913); N J Holloway (1914); A P Freeman (1933); D V P Wright (1947);
G Tribe (1958) and D Underwood (1973).

The two best analyses are:

6-8	J. T. Hearne	South of England	v	Australians	1896
8-9	D Underwood	Kent	v	Sussex	1973

Wickets in a Match

15 (7-84 and 8-119) D V P Wright Kent v Sussex 1947

14 in a match have been taken by: J T Hearne (1896); W C Smith (1913);
A P Freeman (1933); A D G Matthews (1937) and D Underwood (1967).

Hat-Trick

The hat-trick has been achieved by: J Beaumont for South v North 1889,
D V P Wright for Kent v Sussex 1947, and J C Laker for P F Warner's XI v
South 1947.

All-Round Play

117	and	1-8 and 8-52	F E Woolley	Kent	v	Sussex	1910
115	and	5-53 and 3-30	A Drake	Yorkshire	v	Sussex	1911
73 & 11	and	6-65 and 6-59	M W Tate	Sussex	v	Kent	1926
94	and	6-20 and 5-26	A W Greig	Sussex	v	Kent	1972
51 & 81	and	5-25 and 3-35	C M Wells	Sussex	v	Kent	1984

A Few Extras

1886

When the Australians played the South of England, the first ball could not
be bowled until 1 o'clock because their train from London was late. In the
same match play had to be stopped early one evening because shadows
from the houses were reaching the pitch.

1919

When batting for Sussex against Lancashire in 1919 A H H Gilligan missed a ball from R Tyldesley, and, assuming that it had bowled him, walked out. The notes of the Sussex scorer read: 'The scorers saw the wicket-keeper, Boddington, break the wicket, and Mr Gilligan came out, so they assumed that he was stumped. Mr Gilligan, beaten by the ball, and hearing a fielder say 'Well bowled', looked round, saw the bails on the ground, thought he had been bowled, and came out'. Umpire Blake at square leg later said that there was no question of any stumping, so although Gillligan appears in the book as 'stumped Boddington, b Tyldesley . . . 27', he was really never out at all. He should have been recalled.

1929

J B Hobbs (Surrey) was dismissed in *both* innings as:

st Cornford, b Wensley 18
st Cornford, b Wensley 28

1930

When he scored 106 for Surrey Jack Hobbs had now scored centuries against every county in both home and away matches.

1934

F Warne, an Australian leg-breaker bowler making his debut for Worcestershire, bowled three consecutive wides in his 2nd over. His 2nd and 3rd overs read: 4www 2 . . . w4.42. He pitched on the off and his massive breaks turned out of reach.

1936

In the Hampshire second innings when W L Creese had scored 5 an unsuccessful appeal for lbw was made against him. He neglected however to step back into his ground, and J H Parks, fielding the ball in the slips, ran up and broke the wicket, so Creese was 'run out'.

1953

R G Marlar changed arms to bowl the last ball of the match left-handed to J H Wardle, a Yorkshire left-handed batsman, who completed the joke by turning round and batting right-handed to this ball.

1957

Though the pitch was easy, this Sussex v Glamorgan match produced the dreariest batting ever seen at Hastings, and at the end of the second day W Wooller in some protest bowled five underarm deliveries to his rival captain, R G Marlar. There had been some ill-feeling in the previous year's match at Hove.

1958

Every other of the counties had now visited Hastings when Derbyshire made their first appearance there.

1966

According to Alan Oakman, M J K Smith, the Warwickshire captain, gave strict instructions to the team not to risk the slightest chance of being run out. With his own score at 24, he was taken by surprise and run out by Peter Ledden, who had one of the best throwing arms in the country.

Envoi

The sea is near: the channel winds blow up from the west and bring the screaming gulls: they swoop on to the outfield until a ball flurries them away. There is shelter in this enclosed arena with its terraced walls of houses, and the slanting sunlight shines back off the distant windows. High above, the ruined castle looks down upon this intimate oasis of peace amid the busy town.

But not for long now . . .

I cannot be the only one who feels that the passing of this unique ground hurts like the loss of a dear friend.

GB

Colin Cowdrey

Bibliography

Books consulted include:

John Manwaring Baines *Historic Hastings* F J Parsons 1955
Anthony Belt (editor) *Hastings Past and Present*, K Saville 1937
Gerald Brodribb *The Croucher*, London Magazine Editions 1974
Gerald Brodribb *Maurice Tate*, London Magazine Editions 1976
Gerald Brodribb *Next Man In*, Pelham Books 1985
Dudley Carew *England Over*, Martin Secker 1927
Denis Compton *Playing for England*, Sampson Low, Marston 1948
Henry Cousins *Hastings of Bygone Days and the Present*, Parsons 1911
A E R Gilligan *Sussex Cricket*, Chapman & Hall 1933
G L Jessop *A Cricketer's Log*, Hodder & Stoughton 1922
John Mulvaney & Rex Harcourt *Cricket Walkabout*, Macmillan 1988
James Phillips *Hastings & St Leonards Cricket Club*, Parsons 1894
David Sheppard *Parson's Pitch*, Hodder & Stoughton 1964
Alfred D Taylor *Hastings Cricket Festival 1887-1903*, Parsons 1903
G Washer *Sussex Cricket 1728-1957*, Sussex CC Club 1957
also: *Wisden Cricketers' Almanack*
        Hastings & St Leonards Observer